Laura M. Huchton

PROTECT YOUR CHILD

A Parent's Safeguard Against Child Abduction and Sexual Abuse

A SPECTRUM BOOK

PRENTICE-HALL, INC., Englewood Cliffs, New Jersey 07632

Library of Congress Cataloging in Publication Data

Huchton, Laura M. (Laura Marie)
   Protect your child.

   "A Spectrum Book."
   Bibliography: p.
   Includes index.
   1. Child molesting—United States—Prevention.
2. Abduction—United States—Prevention. 3. Missing
children—United States. 4. Safety education—
United States. I. Title.
HQ72.U53H83 1985   362.7'044   85-3393
ISBN 0-13-731456-6
ISBN 0-13-731449-3 (pbk.)

10 9 8 7 6 5 4 3 2 1

ISBN 0-13-731456-6

ISBN 0-13-731449-3 {PBK.}

Editorial/production supervision by Joyce Levatino
Cover design by Hal Siegel
Manufacturing buyer: Carol Bystrom

This book is available at a special discount when ordered in
bulk quantities. Contact Prentice-Hall, Inc., General
Publishing Division, Special Sales, Englewood Cliffs, N.J. 07632.

Prentice-Hall International (UK) Limited, *London*
Prentice-Hall of Australia Pty. Limited, *Sydney*
Prentice-Hall Canada Inc., *Toronto*
Prentice-Hall Hispanoamericana, S.A., *Mexico*
Prentice-Hall of India Private Limited, *New Delhi*
Prentice-Hall of Japan, Inc., *Tokyo*
Prentice-Hall of Southeast Asia Pte. Ltd., *Singapore*
Whitehall Books Limited, *Wellington, New Zealand*
Editora Prentice-Hall do Brasil Ltda., *Rio de Janeiro*

For

*Timmy, Dwayne, Paul, Will, Everett, Garrett, Janie,
Wendy, Lacy, Katie, Carrie, Christon, Emily, Jeremy,
Joshua, Eric, Anita, Ashlee, Paige, Joy, and John.*

May your journeys through childhood be safe and happy.

Contents

VITAL INFORMATION

MISSING: WHAT TO DO?

Preface

I could tell you stories that would break your heart. I could tell you stories that would horrify you because they horrified me. I could show you pictures of missing and murdered children that would haunt you forever. They will haunt me forever. In writing this book, there have been times when I had to lock the pictures and stories away in my desk. I could not write my way through the tears they caused.

There is no way to take you through the empty rooms of missing children. You cannot see their toys gathering dust on the shelf or reach out to give a missing child's grieving parent a hug. I cannot take you into an emergency room to hear the terrified cries of a molested child.

There is much that you can do, however. Learn to protect your children now. Love them enough to train them. Care for them enough to become involved in local, state, and federal decisions that will concern them.

Keep your children from becoming the next statistic. You *can* make the difference.

Acknowledgments

The writing of this book has been made possible through the encouragement and cooperation of many people: Lois

McHargue, Tim Huchton, Lenny Cavallero, Betty Casey, President Ezra Taft Benson of The Church of Jesus Christ of Latter-Day Saints, Bishop Roger Bonnett of The Church of Jesus Christ of Latter-Day Saints, Joseph Bongiorno of The Orlando, Florida, Police Department, Bill Carter of the Federal Bureau of Investigation (NCIC), John and Louise Clinkscales of Find-Me, Inc., Betty DiNova of The Dee Scofield Awareness Program, Yolanda Rodriguez-Escobar of the Texas Department of Human Resources, Bill Hawes of Puppet Productions, Inc., Patti Linebaugh of SLAM (Society's League Against Molestation), June Vlasity of The Society for Young Victims, and John Walsh of The Adam Walsh Child Resource Center and The National Center for Missing and Exploited Children.

Throughout this book, the names of victims and their families have been changed for their protection and privacy. In some instances, as requested by parents of victims, circumstances have been altered.

Introduction

It was a bright spring day when ten-year-old Susan tearfully crawled from a drainage ditch and limped to a neighbor's home to phone her mother.

Her mother remembers the day vividly:

"When Susan called me she was hysterical. I knew something had happened, but I thought she had just fallen off of her bike and skinned her knee.

"I went to pick her up and she ran to the car and crawled on the floor. She cried, 'Don't let anyone see me' and then pointed to her shorts. They were covered with blood."

Susan had ridden her bike to a nearby grocery store. She was followed and brutally raped.

She became one of a growing list of hundreds of thousands of child sexual-assault victims. It is estimated that for every reported case of child sexual abuse, there may be nine others left unreported.

National experts estimate that one out of every four girls and one out of every ten boys will be sexually molested by the time they reach adulthood. This grim picture becomes even more dismal when taking the number of missing children into account. There may be as many as a million vanished children per year.

One of the most painful tasks of parenthood is coming face

to face with the dangers that await children daily. Realizing that they can no longer allow their children to curiously roam in public areas or even their own neighborhoods places a heavy burden of concern upon parents.

This concern and the fact that as a child I was molested prompted the beginning of *Protect Your Child*.

The test that you will find in this book was developed from hundreds of accounts of crimes against children. Additional research information was contributed by such remarkable organizations as: SLAM (Society's League Against Molestation), Find-Me, Inc., and the Dee Scofield Awareness Program, Inc.

The unique two-part comprehensive safety program begins with a written exam that can be offered to preschoolers as an oral test. It then progresses to a multi-stage skills test in which each level of required skills is progressively more difficult to master than the last.

Stage I (Basic Skills) involves simple tests that create an environment of safety awareness between a parent and child. A parent is required to establish a pattern of communication with his or her child by discussing the child's activities. Parents must watch for signs of careless independence that could lead to the child's being sexually abused or abducted.

Stage II (Intermediate Skills) puts the child to work, learning the use of certain types of telephones and observing potentially threatening situations.

Stage III (Advanced Skills) deals with obviously threatening situations and tests a child's ability to calculate the risk and act accordingly.

Although there are no guarantees that can be offered for a child's personal safety, *Protect Your Child* will do more to train a child than any other book available. Safety training is the first line of defense for the most precious resource this country has—its children.

PART ONE

RECOGNIZING THE PROBLEM

Chapter 1

There Is No Such Thing as Overprotection

There is no such thing as an overprotective parent or an over-trained child—especially today when there is some dispute among authorities on child safety as to whether the number of missing children per year is in the hundreds or thousands or soaring into the millions. This statistical range does not include the number of children who are sexually abused. The one area on which all organizations will agree is that we do have a serious problem with crimes perpetrated against children.

At first glance, it appears that parents are only now discovering that the perils in the world can reach out to destroy their own children. Yet perils have always existed, to one degree or another, plaguing generations who have mourned and wept for their abused and murdered young.

Vulnerable and bewildered by the dangers that lure children away, parents search for answers to their questions about the future:

- What can I do to protect my child?
- What is the law doing to protect and help child victims of sexual abuse and abduction?
- Will these problems continue to exist or even worsen, regardless of government intervention?

- What are the schools in my community doing to protect children?
- Is my child safe anywhere anymore?
- Where can I turn for help if I need it?

Protect Your Child gives you much of the basic information that you as a parent need in order to reach valuable sources of help. Advice and information from widely scattered child safety organizations and from parents of missing and murdered children are offered in this book. Yet even with help from such interested persons as these, there are no magical solutions or guarantees that can be given by anyone concerning your child's safety. However, coupled with your own efforts, this book will provide an excellent training program for you and your child. There are no get-safe-quick methods used here. It is your responsibility to take needed time to train and explain, but your time will be well spent and may save the lives of young loved ones.

Childhood dangers such as sexual abuse, abduction, and murder are a commonplace reality. The existence of child-related crime has been rarely acknowledged in the past. Generations of parents remained blind to the problems in part because they felt it to be a shameful subject. Yet through their ignorance and disbelief the problem has grown like a fulminating virus into gigantic proportions.

It is only since parents have begun seeking answers and demanding action that the frightening truths are surfacing. Information on a wide range of subjects including pedophiles (adults sexually attracted to children), child prostitution, pornography, and molestation is becoming a daily topic of conversation. Newspapers, magazines, and television programs are filled with the harsh realities of child sexual abuse. Yet it is because of their frank coverage of the subject that parents are now keenly aware of the risk to which children are subjected on a daily basis.

No longer is the child-molesting pedophile thought to be a total stranger. It is more likely that he or she is a familiar figure within the family or the community. Such people are not likely to be poorly dressed but can be fashionably outfitted and of any age or occupation. Attraction to children will cause them to be drawn to their activities like a moth to light.

Hundreds of pornography magazines and films, a great many of which involve children, are available in this country. The pedophile, who is well fed by this unending source of gratification, is likely to be incited by this material to further his criminal acts against children.

Thus parents must be watchful of all children, from babies in arms to teenagers. The job of guardianship can be burdensome. Children of all ages are targets for pornography, prostitution, and sexual abuse such as molestation or rape. Those who are dealt these abuses within the family unit may join the vast number of runaways, many of whom each year end up in unidentified graves. Others simply vanish, never to be heard from again.

Although most parents agree that teaching safety is a worthwhile endeavor, they lack the vital information needed to educate themselves and train their children. The following pages provide parents with important discussion material. The points covered are elaborated on in Part Two of *Protect Your Child.*

FOUR SPECIAL WORDS
FOR PARENTS

Parents must learn to control their anxiety level to minimize transferring concerns to their children. A child does not need to hear a descriptive account of what can happen if he or she doesn't learn the safety rules. Such tactics create a negative environment for learning.

Parents should not safety train if either the child or parent is under stress. A four-word reminder, *Safety Training Is Fun,* should be taped in a prominent place and used frequently. A stress-free environment creates an optimal learning experience for children.

FOUR SPECIAL WORDS
FOR CHILDREN

Just as parents need to be reminded to control their anxieties in training, children also must be taught to *Remember Your Safety Rules*.

These four words pertain to all vital information that the child learns. Before the child goes outdoors to play or off to catch the school bus, state the reminder clearly and firmly. Children can repeat the rules that apply to them during their activities for the day.

Colorful letters can be cut and taped in a child's room as a reminder that safety rules must never be forgotten.

SPECIFIC SAFETY TOPICS

Sergeant Frederick L. Whitley of the crime prevention section of the San Antonio Police Department recommends the following safety topics for parents.

Stranger Awareness

Teaching children about strangers can be difficult if the child is very young. Usually, the older the child, the more cognizant of strangers he or she will be. By age four a child can be taught the difference between a stranger and a trusted family friend. The child can also be taught to spot strangers by playing the Stranger Game in the skills test in Part Two.

Because most children have some misconception about what a stranger is, it is reasonable to teach them that their ideas are not always realistic. You must make the point clearly that a stranger is anyone that your child or your family does not know extremely well.

Police and child safety organizations suggest that children should be taught these basic principles of stranger awareness:

- A stranger can be male or female.
- A stranger can be young or old.
- A stranger can be well dressed and drive a fine automobile, van, or truck.
- A stranger can be dirty and poorly dressed and drive an old car, van, or truck.
- Children should never be involved with strangers in any way.
- Children should never accept rides with anyone, even a friend, unless given direct parental permission. Just because you know someone does not mean you are safe with that person.
- There are good strangers and bad strangers, but children cannot tell the difference.

Safety Away from Home

A basic list of rules for mall shopping follows:

- When you shop in a mall, remember this simple rule: You have *less* control of the circumstances in a large place, so you must have *more* control of your children.
- Do not take a large group of children into a shopping mall. As a general rule, take only those children you can keep your hands on.
- *Keep your hands on your children.* Be sure that they accompany you into dressing rooms or wherever you go. If they need to use the bathroom, never allow them to go alone. It is best that you accompany them.
- Be aware of too much window shopping. You can easily become distracted and end up with a missing child.
- Teach your children the Mall Game. Take them into a shopping mall, and let them make five choices of whom they would go to if

they were lost. Write their answers down and discuss them. Next, walk through the mall and point out persons you would prefer they go to for help. In each instance, make the point clear that they should go to someone who works in a store. Point out name tags or uniforms that would identify a store worker or security guard. Then go a step further and introduce your child to the worker, asking how he or she would help a lost child. The last step is to ask your children clearly and firmly if they fully understand what you expect them to do should they become lost.

- Do not impose upon clerks or anyone else to babysit for you while you shop.
- Never send a child into a video arcade alone while you shop. Pimps, pushers, and pornographers may be waiting to take advantage of them there.
- Be aware of others.
- A mall is an excellent place to teach youngsters to spot strangers.

If these basic rules are followed, they can help to keep your children safe while you are shopping in a mall. A young west Texas mother shares her story:

That day in the mall was the most frightening of my life. I had been shopping, walking around looking in the windows, when I turned around and noticed that my son wasn't there. I called him and he didn't come. I was so scared that I felt sick. I started to run, looking through every store. I begged the clerks to help me. They probably thought I was crazy.

I was running toward the exit when I noticed a man dressed in a suit. He had Jeremy almost out the door. I screamed and ran full power and grabbed him just before he was out. The man took off running and was never caught.

That night when I was tucking Jeremy into bed he looked up and said that the man was real nice and had given him a cookie. Then he asked me why I was crying. It was right then that I realized I had never taught him anything about safety because I didn't know anything about it.

Car Safety

A grandmother relates a near-tragic account of a day at the grocery store:

> *I had just a few things to pick up at the store for my daughter so I left my grandsons Jeff and John in the car. Jeff was 12 then and could easily take care of John, who was just barely two. I didn't think to roll up the windows or lock the doors because we live in such a small town. Nothing had ever happened to children there so I wasn't concerned.*
>
> *When I got back to the car, Jeff and John were crying and holding each other. Jeff said that after I left a woman came up and started talking to them through the car window. Then she tried to grab John and pull him out of the window. Jeff pulled the baby one way, and the woman pulled him the other. Finally, a few people stopped to watch, and the woman ran. She was never caught. That day I was cured of leaving children in the car.*

Children should *never* be left in cars, even locked ones. A serious assailant is not deterred by a locked door. He or she can easily trick a child into opening the door or use other means of gaining entry.

Grocery Shopping

Remember the following rules when grocery shopping:

- Don't allow children to speak to strangers, even if they pay special compliments to you or your child.
- Don't turn your back on your child for any reason.
- Never send a child to get an item you forgot to pick up.
- Take only as many children *as you can safely keep your hands on.*
- Buy them a bakery cookie or something to occupy their time and keep them from wandering.
- Never send a bored child alone to the toy department or anywhere else.

- Be sure children are seated safely in the grocery cart or on it.
- Older children can be kept busy (and near) by pushing the cart.
- Do not allow children to walk more than three feet away from you.
- Do not leave your child in the basket at the checkout stand while you go to pick up a forgotten item. Store clerks cannot be responsible for the safety of your child.
- Try to leave children with a reliable babysitter on shopping days. Check Mothers' Day Out programs offered by local churches.

School

The following rules apply especially to school situations:

- Police departments and child safety organizations recommend that parents know the exact path their children walk to school. Point out offices or homes the child could run into if help was needed. If a home has a child aid sticker in the window, such as that of the Helping Hand, be sure to stop and meet the family. Almost anyone can obtain such stickers. You must be sure the family is legitimately concerned for the children's welfare.
- Check with your school to see if absentee reporting is in effect. If not, visit a PTA meeting and bring up the subject. Parents of children who do not show up in class have the right to know about it immediately. It is imperative that this program be established in every school for the sake of any abducted child. Precious hours that could be used to alert authorities and search for the child are lost because schools do not take the initiative to institute this program.
- Encourage your school to begin a fingerprinting program.
- Never give blanket permission for a school to take your children away from school grounds. You have the right to know where your child is at all times.
- On the rare occasion that you refuse to grant permission for your child to attend a school function off school grounds, find out what provisions have been made for your child, exactly who will care for him or her, and where your child will be during the function.

- If an off-grounds school activity is planned, find out the exact time and place. If you feel that there is reason to be concerned, call the place and verify that the school is taking your children there.

- Know your children's teachers and coaches.

- In the event of an off-grounds school activity, find out who the student chaperones will be. Chaperones should be faculty members and the students' parents.

- Be a volunteer parent, willing to help teachers, coaches, or scout leaders.

- Attend all your child's after-school sports, civic activities, or classes. If you cannot be present, ask a family member or a trusted friend to be there. If this is not possible, hire a reliable sitter to cover the event for you and watch your child.

- Parents of Girl and Boy Scouts should be sure to carefully check arrangements for overnight campouts. Children away from home overnight can be especially vulnerable to molesters. A parent should always be welcome to accompany a group on a campout because scout organizations are dependent on volunteers. If you are not welcome by the leader, be sure to investigate.

- Parents should be involved in planning committees in scouting and other activities. A caring parent can make the difference between a safe trip and a possibly tragic one.

A police lieutenant in a small Texas community reports this story of a sexual offender who made repeated attempts to get children into his car near the elementary school ground.

Both times the molester approached seven- to twelve-year-old boys on bikes. He told them that their mother had had an accident and was in the hospital and that he would take them there. But he was never successful. The parent reaction to these attempts was tremendous! The parents got together in the P.T.O. (Parent Teacher Organization) and got all the details from the police. Then they made up flyers with the information for each child to take home. After that, many parents began picking up their children at school.

Religious Meetings

Some rules for attending places of worship are:

- Children have a tendency to scatter quickly after a Sunday School or religious meeting. Ask your child's teacher to keep the child after class so that you can pick up him or her.
- Know your child's Sunday School teachers and youth activity directors.
- Make surprise visits to class.
- If you have a child in the nursery, be certain the nursery workers are competent. Check their background with church supervisors.
- Never leave a baby or child of nursery age in a poorly equipped or dirty nursery. This is an instant indication of poor care on the part of the attendants and the church.
- Be sure the nursery is on the checklist to be inspected by church authorities.
- Make surprise nursery visits.
- If you have any doubts about leaving your child in the care of a Sunday School teacher or nursery attendant, then don't.
- Report any and all incidents that attest to poor care on the part of the staff.
- Do not allow your children on the church parking lot or anywhere outside without you.
- If you intend to leave your child, volunteer to help overburdened nursery attendants in any way necessary, even if it means your missing a class.

An incident reported by a police department indicates that it is wise for parents to be cautious of their children when they are in a church:

> A member called and reported that she saw this fellow fondling one of the kids. . . . His method of operation was to get involved in a church in some type of leadership position involving youth. He was arrested, and we found that he had been in the penitentiary for the same thing.

Public Restrooms

Rules for you to follow when your child must use a public restroom include the following:

- If possible, always accompany your child to a public restroom. When a boy becomes too old to accompany his mother to the ladies' restroom, she can stand outside the door of the men's restroom and wait for him.
- Fathers may knock on the door of the ladies' restroom to clear it before taking their daughter inside.
- If your child goes unaccompanied to a public restroom and you become worried, you can always call through the door to see if he or she is all right. If there is no answer, enter and make certain that all is well.
- Store managers, restaurant owners, or other staff will be happy to oblige a concerned parent by checking on the child in a restroom if the parent does not want to enter.

Public Swimming Pools

Pedophiles are attracted to the places where children congregate. Be certain you follow these simple rules:

- Don't let the lifeguards become babysitters. It's not their job.
- Warn your child about the potential dangers of a dressing room. Sexual offenders could be waiting for children to enter alone. Accompany your child if possible. If you cannot accompany your child to a swimming pool, have a trusted friend or family member do so.
- Beware of watchful strangers, as in any other situation.

Parks and Playgrounds

Parks and playgrounds are almost never supervised. They are a perfect place for sexual offenders to wait for unaccompanied children.

- If you cannot accompany your child, have a responsible adult do so.
- Do not allow a child to enter a park or playground restroom alone. An adult whom you trust should take the child in.
- In large parks and playgrounds it is easy for children to wander. Parents should stay within their child's chosen play area.

Drive-in and Walk-in Movies

Accompany children to movie theaters. If you cannot go, be sure another parent or responsible adult attends. Also:

- Follow the rules for public restrooms.
- Teach your children to run to an authority figure (an usher, manager, or ticket seller) to report incidents.
- Children can easily be enticed with candy or other bribes to leave the theater from the back exit. Be sure they are alerted to this potential danger.
- Teach your child to scream and run for help should he or she be molested in any public place such as a movie theater. If you must sacrifice in order to see a movie with your children then do so. Viewing what your child sees on screen may help you to direct him or her to better choices, and the safety benefit can offset any sacrifice you may have to make in order to accompany your child.

THE DOCTOR'S OFFICE, EMERGENCY ROOM, OR HOSPITAL

Rules parents should be aware of when going to the doctor's office:

- At least one parent should remain with the child at all times.
- You have the right to question all procedures and require a full explanation from the doctor about his medical choices in your

child's behalf. If you are concerned about any medical treatment, do not depend on a nurse's explanation. Ask the doctor.

- If you are concerned about the medications your child is being given, you have a right to question the doctor. You do not have to accept a nurse's explanation.

- You have a right to refuse all treatment and medications that are ordered for your child, but do not act hastily. Remember that a qualified doctor should know the proper procedures to follow in order to help your child.

HOME SECURITY: DOGS

A healthy, protective, barking dog can be a great deterrent to crime against children. However, a parent cannot expect a dog to become a permanent babysitter. Nor can a dog be depended upon to actually attack in the case of a child's being molested. Dogs can be bribed, drugged, shot, or poisoned in an assailant's serious attempt to harm a child. Yet, on the whole, they are one of the best possible means of alerting and protecting children.

Many excellent breeds of dogs are well known for their alertness and their ability to protect, but ranking among the most watchful and competent are the larger breeds, such as Doberman pinschers and German shepherds. Dog trainers have made guard or attack dogs available to the general public, and some dogs are specifically trained to be protectors of young children. If you consider buying such a dog, check the trainer's background carefully to be sure he or she is competent and has a good reputation. Ask for referrals from owners to whom the trainer has sold dogs. Then be positive that your child and the dog are completely compatible. Children should have an opportunity to make regular visits to a guard dog before it is allowed to come home.

Try the dog for its ability to protect the child before you

leave the training area. The following story is related by a father of three:

I saw the ad in the paper for protection dogs. We had been robbed a couple of times when we had been away from home on vacation, so I thought a guard dog would come in handy.

I really didn't buy the dog for my girls, even though they liked him a lot. But I took Nancy, our oldest daughter, with me to check out the trainer. We were impressed with the place. It was a clean barn filled with big cages with a dog in each one. There were Dobermans and shepherds. They were really something—beautiful, you know. The trainer was a nice guy, and he was convinced that one of his dogs could protect my daughter. I told him that I didn't need a dog for that kind of protection. It had never occurred to me that the girls needed to be looked after that way. I told him that I just wanted a good dog to watch after the house. So we walked around and he quoted prices. I had no idea that a dog could cost so much money. I thought it was ridiculous and told Nancy we could go to the pound and find a decent dog for $40 or $50. The trainer agreed that we could do that, but a pound dog couldn't be proven as a protector as his dogs could. So I asked him to show me, and he did.

We walked down to an arena where a trainer, called an agitator, was working with a dog. He had a padded cover over his arm, and this Doberman was attacking. It was really amazing to watch. They would give the dog a command and he would attack and retreat. It sold me right away. So we went back to the barn and picked out the dog we wanted. It practically wiped out our savings account to get that dog.

About a month later, my wife and I went out and left Nancy in charge of her little sisters. She was fourteen then, plenty old enough to babysit. We said goodbye and told them when we would be back. An hour later the girls went out to feed the dog. They played with him a while, then decided to walk him to a neighbor's house to show him off. While they were on the way, walking on the sidewalk, a van pulled up and followed them. Nancy said the dog growled when a man tried to talk to them through the window. He got out of the van and did not act scared of the dog. The little girls ran into a neighbor's yard and left Nancy holding the dog, but everything turned out all right! Even without a command, the dog jumped the guy when he made a move for Nancy, and she said that dog almost tore him to pieces.

When she gave him the off command, he quit right away, and the girls ran to the neighbors to call the police.

Important points to remember about your dog are the following:

- Keep your dog in excellent health. Consult a vet when it seems ill or needs shots.

- Illness or injury will limit the dog's ability to use its senses keenly. A dog that is free from illness can devote its energy to protecting your family.

- Encourage your dog to bark with discrimination. A dog that barks constantly is of little use for warning the family of impending danger. A dog that barks to alert the family of the advances of others is doing its job.

- A dog should not be used as a babysitter. Ultimately, parents are always responsible for their child.

- Dogs are not infallible. They can be tricked and killed.

- A dog cannot always be expected to attack to protect a child.

- Check the credentials of guard dog trainers. Ask for referrals.

- If you plan to buy a guard dog, be certain your child and the dog are compatible. Some dogs do not like children, and no amount of training can change their preferences.

- Before you take a protection dog home, have it tried for its ability to protect your child. If your child is old enough, allow him or her to walk with the dog and give it simple commands under the guidance of a trainer. When an older child is allowed to have a protection dog, the child should be trained to handle and care for it properly.

- Never allow a child to mistreat a guard dog (or any other animal, for that matter) in any way.

- Teach your child to listen to the dog's signals of danger: growling, ears perked forward, tenseness in posture, and advances toward people are possible warnings that trouble is near.

PARENT-CHILD DISTRESS WORDS

An emergency distress word can be any word that is agreed upon by parent and child. The child may prefer an unusual animal name, the unique name of a place or person, a shape, or a color.

Explain that the distress word must remain a secret from everyone because if used properly it could save the child's life. It is a word that indicates that there is danger present. Distress words can indicate whether a child should trust someone or not.

Michael's Special Word

Michael's family, like many families throughout the country, uses an emergency distress word. The word can be used in a variety of ways, as Michael's father explains:

> We heard about distress words for children five and a half years ago. It made good sense to us to help protect our son in this way. Our distress word has changed now, so I can tell you that before we changed it the word was "Mad Hatter."

> We use our distress word in many ways. When we leave Michael with a babysitter, we call to be sure everything is okay. If Michael says his distress word, then we return home because we know there is trouble.

> Occasionally we exchange the word with someone outside of the family. That can make things much more complicated, but it's handy if you have to depend on someone else to pick up your child. If a third person says the distress word and Michael knows that it has been planned, then he will go with that person.

> Once, when Michael was in nursery school, a mother called to invite him to her daughter's birthday party. We were familiar with the mother and checked with the school to be sure everything was clear with them. They verified her story and gave her a fine recommendation, telling us that she planned to pick up five of the children in her daughter's class and take them to her home for the party. After further discussion with her, we agreed to give our permission.

At the appointed time, she drove to the school and picked up the children. I had forgotten to explain the distress word to her, so when she arrived at the school, Michael refused to get in her car. When he asked for his word, she was very confused and made one up. Michael sensed there was something wrong and ran into the school to tell his teacher. The teacher told him it was all right to get into the car, but he insisted on hearing the distress word or he would not go. Finally the teacher called our home, and we gave Michael personal permission to get into the car. Later the mother called us. She was so impressed with Michael's actions that she now uses special distress words for her children.

A breakdown of Michael's action is beneficial in teaching the importance of distress words. First, Michael's parents used the word to protect their child. They never let it slip to anyone else. Michael was taught that the word was a secret and that parents are the only ones who should ask a child to keep a secret. He agreed that the word would be chosen from his favorite book, *Alice in Wonderland.*

Another impressive point in the story was that Michael was only five when he first began using distress words. Such words, although they will change through the years, will become a natural safety law for a child to follow throughout childhood and adolescence. Each time a distress word is exchanged with someone outside the family, the word must be changed for the protection of the child.

Distress words may be used in many ways. For instance, as Michael's father adds, if children are left with a babysitter, you will want to call home and check on them. Remember to talk to your child, not the babysitter. Every child should know that if he feels frightened or in danger, he should use the distress word. Should he slip his word into the conversation, verify it by briefly asking him if he is in trouble. If he answers affirmatively, hang up and get home as fast as you can. If you feel that there is a real possibility of danger and you cannot get home quickly enough, call the police and explain the situation to them. They will be happy to oblige a concerned parent. Be patient if your child misuses his distress word at first. He will become familiar and comfortable with it in time. Then, like any new experience, it will become second nature with practice.

WHEN YOUR CHILD ANSWERS THE DOOR

Parents who neglect to lock doors usually have children who neglect to lock doors. Although a locked door may not keep a professional thief out of your house, it is a deterrent for the criminal who depends on people to leave doors open or to let him or her inside. A locked door puts space between the assailant and the potential victim, providing the victim with time to reach a source of help.

Teach your children to answer a knock on your door with caution. Too often they race wildly to see if they can beat brothers and sisters to let a visitor inside. Discourage this practice. Set safety rules and follow them when answering the door. Some rules for answering the door are:

- Police suggest that children who are left at home alone or with a babysitter not answer a knock on the door.
- Parents must decide exactly what instructions they wish children to follow if:
  - A knocker persists.
  - A knocker is persistent, then goes away and returns.
  - A knocker claims to be in distress and needs to use the telephone.
  - The knocker is a friend or family member, yet an unexpected caller.
  - The knocker tries to carry on a conversation with the child through the door.

Many parents feel that a persistent knocker is a potential threat when they are absent from home. They give their children directions to call the police in any one of the foregoing situations, except when family members visit. One parent suggests this procedure:

> We tape a picture of a bad-looking stranger on the door before we leave home. This reminds the babysitter and our children never to open the door, regardless of how friendly a person sounds. If there is a persistent knocker, the kids know to call the police. We don't even let them invite friends in when we are gone. Too many bad things have happened to kids in our neighborhood.

Police may be asked to send a patrol car by your home if you are planning to leave your children alone or with a babysitter. The police crime prevention department will usually provide free home inspections, giving suggestions on different types of peepholes and locks for doors and windows. Such advice can prove to be very valuable, even life saving.

The cheapest way to save a life can be by setting an example. Keep your doors locked day and night. Train your children to follow exact instructions concerning answering the door. Remember to reward them when they act accordingly.

WHEN YOUR CHILD ANSWERS THE TELEPHONE

Every child should know exactly how to use the telephone. Children should know how to use all types of phones, not just the one at home. They should be taught to use cordless, dial, punch-button, and pay phones. Then, in an emergency, the child will know how to use any available phone.

Home phones should have a colorful illustrated list of emergency numbers taped to them. A police hat can be drawn by the number for the police, a fire hat or truck for the fire department, and so on. These should be covered in plastic to keep them clean and to prevent damage from moisture.

Almost all children enjoy the privilege of using the family phone. They should be made aware, however, that child molesters can use the phone to obtain information for the purposes of harming children. It is best from the start that each child know the safe methods of answering a caller's questions.

Most callers will ask a child if the parents are at home. For instance, they will ask for the mother to come to the phone. Often a child will say, "She is not at home right now." The caller can then ask for the father to come to the phone, and a typical reply might be, "He's not here either." The caller now has the first valuable piece of information. The child is without the usual source of protection. The parents are not at home. It is an easy step now to ask, "May I speak to your babysitter?" The reply might be, "I'm too old for a babysitter; there's nobody here but me." Now the caller is sure there are no adults present. All he or she needs to know is, "Do you know when your parents will be back?"

It is remarkably easy for callers to get almost any kind of information they want from a child. This certainly puts the child in a vulnerable position. A molester can easily gain access to children who are left untrained and unaccompanied by parents. The chances are that if children aren't taught to use the phone correctly, they might also let a visitor inside. The visitor could be dangerous.

Children sometimes argue that they know everyone who calls on the phone and consider them to be friends. The absolute rule of phone safety is that the child cannot differentiate between friend and foe and must treat every caller the same. It is important to make your children aware that family, friends, and even neighbors can be child molesters. A molester can be extremely persuasive and charming over the telephone. Reinforce this idea: Regardless of the caller's use of pleasant conversation or even coercion, the child must never allow the caller to know that he or she is at home without parents or some other protector.

An approach similar to the following is a safe response for the child:

Caller: Hi, how are you today?
Child: Fine.

Caller: May I speak to your Dad or Mom?

Child: My parents can't come to the phone right now. They asked me to take a message. They will call you in a few minutes. What is your name and phone number?

The child should then contact the parents and give them the message. Parents must return the call and check to be sure the caller was legitimate. If parents cannot reach such a name or number, however, they should return home at once. In case parents cannot be reached by phone, children should have stand-by numbers of relatives or close friends who can call back on the number. If the caller cannot be reached, it is imperative that some responsible adult go to the house and stay with the child.

Points to remember:

- Whenever a child is left at home alone, he or she must convince all callers that the parents are at home and that they will return a message as soon as they can.

- Children should be taught to use all kinds of phones. Phone Field Days are fun. Parents may take children out for ice cream and to see and use all different types of phones.

- Children should be warned not to carry on phone conversations with a man *or* woman if you are not at home, regardless of how charming or persistent the caller seems to be.

- Regardless of where they are, children have the personal right to call home at any time if they feel afraid.

- If parents leave children at home alone or with a babysitter, they should call home at regular intervals to check on them.

- Parents should bypass the babysitter and speak directly to the child.

- If a child feels afraid or in any kind of danger (even from the babysitter), he or she should use a distress word. Parents should return home or call the police at once if the child uses this word.

- The words "My parents can't come to the phone right now, they asked me to take a message" can be taped above the phone for older children.

CHOOSING THE RIGHT BABYSITTER

Selecting a reliable sitter can be difficult. Parents should exercise caution when they choose a babysitter. The following points are helpful:

- Choose among trusted family members first.
- Choose from trusted friends, preferably those with children, when no family member is available.
- Make reciprocal agreements to trade babysitting time with close friends.
- Friends who have had excellent babysitters can recommend them to you. But, still, check other references.
- The last choice is to leave your child with a stranger. It is always safer to take your child with you than to hand her or his life over to a total stranger. If you have no other choice, be sure to check at least five references and any state registration the babysitter may have. Ask for names of neighbors as extra references. Check with the child welfare or police department of your town to see if there have been any reports of misconduct with a child on the part of the sitter.
- Start a babysitting co-op with other reliable mothers in your community, or simply take your child with you wherever you go. One grandmother has said, "In the days when I was growing up there were no such things as babysitters. We went where our parents went. When there was a party, all the kids came with toys and blankets. Then our parents would put us to bed at the party, and carry us home asleep. We had a delightful time."
- When you leave your child at home, call regularly to check on him or her. Be sure that your child knows to use his distress word if he is in any danger or afraid of anything. Assure your child that you will return home quickly if he uses the word.
- Beware of the babysitter who will not let you talk to your child when you call to check. Do not accept excuses that the child is too busy or playing in the yard. Insist on talking to your child. If you are not allowed to speak to the child, return home at once. Call a neighbor to give a quick check on your child while you are on the way home.

- Provide the babysitter with important information such as emergency phone numbers, safety rules, exits and entrances in case of fire, location of first aid kit, the number where you can be reached, and the type of care you expect your child to be given.

YARD SAFETY

How safe are children in their own yard? Do not assume that just because children are in their own yard they are completely safe. Certain safety rules must be adhered to in order to minimize the danger of the child's being taken from the yard, wandering away, or being sexually assaulted in the yard. When parents cannot be with their children in the yard, it is imperative that the family watch dog be present. A barking dog—the bigger the better—is a good preventive to crime of any kind. But when a watch dog is especially attached to the children in a family, an excellent crime deterrent has been established. Be sure that your child knows never to leave the yard to play or to let the dog out for any reason.

It is equally important to take time to check on children frequently if you cannot stay with them in the yard. Encourage them to report to you on a regular schedule. This method will help to keep them aware of the world outside the play yard and of your expectation that they are to observe neighborhood happenings. They should report anything out of the usual, such as cars passing slowly or individuals who may be watching them play or who try to speak to them.

Children should not be allowed to speak to any strangers who may strike up a conversation. They should be instructed to run, taking younger brothers and sisters with them if such an instance occurs. Once a conversation is begun with a molester, the child can easily become confused or persuaded to do things he or she would not ordinarily do. A young mother confided:

I told them not to talk to anyone outside. I checked on them regularly from the window. But a few minutes later I heard my son's voice. He sounded very excited. As I rushed outside, he was speaking to a stranger on a motorcycle who had stopped for directions. The young man had offered him a ride. I feel I got there just in time, but I'll never leave my kids alone in the yard again.

Make rules for the special time when friends come to join your children in the yard. This is especially difficult because one untrained youngster can lead a whole group of children into a dangerous situation.

Visiting friends should not be allowed to come and go, leading other youngsters with them. Visitors can be called into a brief family counsel where parents discuss the safety rules everyone is expected to obey.

Reciprocal agreements can be made with neighboring parents to cover important safety measures, such as the care parents are expected to give to visiting youngsters.

As long as visitors are in your yard, you should be responsible for their care. When they decide to visit, they should have made all involved parents aware of where they are and when they will return home. Reinforce the rules that no wandering will be tolerated and that older children should be responsible for younger ones.

Briefly, a list of yard rules consists of the following:

- If possible, a parent should be present in the yard with children at all times.
- The family watch dog should be loose in the yard with the children.
- Children should not be allowed to leave the yard to go elsewhere without parental permission.
- A child must never let the family dog out of the yard. The child should know that the dog can warn of impending danger.
- Check on children frequently if you cannot be with them in the yard.
- Children should report to parents on a regular basis if parents cannot be with them while they play.
- Children must be reminded to remain aware of neighborhood

happenings as they play. They should report anything out of the ordinary.

- A child must never speak to an approaching stranger.

- If a stranger strikes up a conversation, children should be instructed to take younger siblings and run into the house to report the incident.

- Visiting children should be made aware of the family safety rules. They should know that wandering away cannot be tolerated.

- Reciprocal agreements can be made between neighboring parents for the safety of all children involved.

- Parents should be responsible for the care and safety of visiting children.

- When children visit, they should have parental permission and be aware of the time when they are expected to return home. This must be approved by both sets of parents.

- Visiting children should be accompanied home by a parent. They should not be allowed to wander home unattended.

Chapter 2

Knowing Your Neighbor Is Not Enough

Parents become complacent when they are busy with their own affairs in the working world. It is easy to trust children to neighbors, believing they would not do harm to youngsters. Yet sadly, there have been cases that indicate parents and children should use caution around neighbors, friends, and sometimes family.

It is a common practice of many parents to send their children to play with friends in the neighborhood. But do the parents know the neighbors to whom they send their child? If so, how long have they known them? Is the neighbor family one whom parents feel they can trust? What makes parents feel as though the family is a well-adjusted and trustworthy one? Has there ever been the slightest indication on the part of the visiting child or his or her friends that there is a problem in the neighbor's home? Have other neighbors reported any type of misconduct by the family, especially by the male members? Do parents know exactly where their children are? If so, how many times have they made surprise visits to check on their child? During the visits, what was observed?

These are basic questions parents should be able to answer before they send their children to play in the neighborhood or to spend the night with a friend.

Sometimes parents feel as though they know their own family members well. Yet within one's own family there can be sexual perversions such as molestation or incest. These complex and confusing situations are devastating, beginning with one simple mistake: The parents trusted their children to others without question.

If parents have even the slightest doubt about the neighbor family, they should never leave the children with that family. Youngsters will sometimes come to parents with enlightening information that could change their thinking about close friends or family. Yet, unfortunately, parents often show disapproval of such reports and cling obstinately to their belief that friends and family are innocent of such dealings. Few things are more damaging to a child than for his parents to accuse him of lying or ignore his report of sexual abuse. It is a rare occurrence for a child to lie about being sexually molested.

Consider this rule above all else: Whenever you have the slightest doubt or uneasy feeling about friends or members of your family, do not leave your child in their care. An aunt reports:

My young niece was left with me for the summer when her parents vacationed in Europe. My children were grown and gone, so the experience of having a little one around again was fun. Soon I felt as protective of her as I did of my own children.

One day I had a meeting that I needed to attend, so I asked a good friend of mine to care for my niece. She seemed happy that I had asked her, so I left Della with her. I was in the middle of that meeting when a feeling suddenly came over me that I should go get Della. I tried to pretend that I didn't feel it, but after a few minutes I couldn't ignore it any longer. To everyone's surprise I stood up and announced I had to leave.

When I arrived at my friend's house, Della was playing in the front yard. I searched the yard for my friend, but she was not outside. I found her merrily chatting away on the phone, not even aware that Della had gone outside to play. Anything could have happened to the child!

ABOUT PICTURE TAKING

Parents should take at least two to three photographs of their child each year. Children age three and under should have their picture taken once every two months because of the physical changes that occur during this period of rapid growth. Both full-face shots and profiles should be included. These can be kept in a personal file folder along with fingerprints and other vital personal information.

The Wrong Kind of Picture Taking

A young mother relates that a day at the park taught her a valuable lesson:

> *It was such a pretty day that I decided to take the girls to the park. They played near the swing sets while I wrote some letters in the car. I had my back turned, intentionally trying to block out the noise they were making.*
>
> *In a few minutes Ashley and Genny ran to me. They were so excited about the nice man who had stopped to take their picture. He had given each of them a sucker and asked where they lived. It startled me a little, but I didn't think of it again until I told my husband, who is a policeman. He told me the department had taken a number of complaints about a man photographing children. The police department felt he might be a child pornographer.*

Children are usually not aware that it can be dangerous to have their picture taken by others because family picture taking is such a casual practice. Warn your children that incidents of photography by strangers must be reported immediately. Explain that although family picture taking is an acceptable practice, there is a type of photography that is unsafe and can be harmful. Child pornographers can circulate through communities taking pictures of children, then relay the photos to others. If a pornographer gains information from a child, he or she can return to find the child again. Pornographers may attempt to involve children in their activities, which can lead to disappearance.

If your child reports such an occurrence, gather the facts calmly. Ask for the following information:

- a complete description of the individuals involved
- a complete description of the vehicles involved
- any distinguishing features of the individuals or vehicles involved
- types of bribes offered, if any
- types of information sought by the photographer

Gather the information in writing before going to the police. Children can be intimidated by the presence of authority and forget vital information. Be sure to file the data in the child's personal file folder (refer to Chapter 7).

POINTS TO REMEMBER

The points in the following list are important to remember when teaching your child safety awareness:

- Let your children know that you are their Best Friend because you love them more than anyone else in the world.
- Explain that adults and children have certain rights, but an adult's right should never overshadow a child's. SLAM (Society's League Against Molestation) advises parents to tell their children that if an adult needs help, the adult should ask another grown person for help—not a child.
- SLAM also warns that grown people should never ask children to keep secrets, yet they are free to ask other adults to do so. The exception to the rule is when parents ask their own children to keep secrets, such as who is getting what for Christmas.
- The less contact children have with adults who ask them for something, the more safe they will remain.

- SLAM advises children to report all requests to keep secrets. This applies to warnings and threats as well.
- Explain that when parents are aware of such incidents they can take necessary action to protect their children.

A PET FOR PAULA— A GIFT OF COINS

A mother of two children shares the following story:

> *It was a Saturday afternoon when Paula came home from the neighbor's house, and I noticed that she was carrying something in a sack. I didn't pay much attention to it, but when I went into her room later, I found her on the bed stroking a little rabbit. I questioned her about it, and she said the neighbor offered her the rabbit because she liked it. It wasn't until later that I found out he had molested her and given her the rabbit to keep her quiet.*

This story emphasizes the importance of parents' questioning gifts their children are given. Normally, gifts are given on special occasions such as Christmas or birthdays. It would be difficult for parents to have to question all gifts. If gifts or money that seem out of the ordinary are given, the incident should be investigated. A brother explains:

> *I remember a time when we were young when my sister came home from school counting these coins she said a teacher gave to her. She was awfully proud of those things. I watched her put about ten of them into a small jar in her room. I asked my folks if I could have an allowance because I wanted money, too. They said "no" and asked where I got the idea that Jeannie had any money. I told them about the coins, but I don't think they believed me. After a couple of weeks she came home with more coins and stuffed them into her jar. I was real curious about why a teacher would give her money. She never answered me, so I asked if I could have some and she told me no. She was saving the coins for a doll. I knew my folks could never afford a doll for her, and I was sure she was serious about having one. She kept bringing money home and before long bought herself a doll. My folks were really shocked. I remember their asking her how she got the money for it.*

When she finally told them, they didn't believe her. A teacher had paid her to keep the secret that he had "touched" her.

The following list is a summary of rules about gifts:

- When gifts or money are given by a person who normally does not acknowledge your child in this way, it is wise to become curious and check into it.
- When a child refuses to talk about a gift or money, find out why.
- Gifts for special occasions should be from close friends and family. If others offer gifts on these days, check into it.
- Be watchful of gifts or money that a child says he or she has earned. Find out what the child did to earn it.
- Be watchful of gifts or money given on days that are not special occasions.
- Halloween is the one special occasion when children may ask for a gift of candy, yet it has become a dangerous time for many children who have been harmed by poisoned treats or objects inside the candy. However, it can still be a day of treats and fun if children are allowed to participate in church, school, or private parties.

PERSONAL IDENTIFICATION

Gone are the days when children could wear their names on their clothing, scribble it all over their school books, and hang it by a string from their bicycle handlebars. We are faced with trying to outmaneuver the child molester, who has taken full advantage of the visible tag. A grandmother explained the circumstances that caused her to realize the danger of name tags:

I watch a lot of TV, so I've heard about child molesters and kidnappers. But we are a black family, and I believed these people just wanted white children. Last Christmas I bought my granddaughter a little pink sweater with her name on it. She was crazy about that sweater and loved to wear it to school.

My daughter-in-law called me a few months later and told me that a man and woman had stopped my granddaughter on her way to school. They called her by name and tried to get her inside their car. I'm sure they saw her name on that sweater. Later the police told us never to let any of the children wear their names on their clothes. They shouldn't even put it on their school books or toys. I can't imagine what this world is coming to when a little girl can't safely wear a sweater with her name on it.

The child who has her or his name printed on clothing or belongings that are easily seen is a target. The visible name makes the molester's job extremely easy. He or she can gain access to the child by calling her or him directly by name. Skillfully, he can confuse the child to the point that she or he believes it is possible that the molester is a long-lost friend. Such an offender can claim to be the child's parents' friend or that he or she was sent by the parents to pick the child up for a ride home.

It is difficult for children to realize that there are others in the world who would really harm them, especially when they are cherished and cared for at home. Yet, the dangers are ever-present and changing so fast that parents and children must remain alert and try to anticipate tricks before those tricks become part of the technique used by offenders. Staying a jump ahead of child molesters is difficult, but it is worthwhile. A proud grandmother explains:

When my grandchildren came to visit, I made each of them an identification card. They were so delighted with their cards that they promised to keep them in their pockets whenever they went out.

One day several months later my son called to tell me that Karen's identification card had really helped her. She was on her way home from school when a man started following her on foot. She ran into the corner grocery and pulled out her card and asked the grocer to call her home number because she was too scared to do it herself. Then she explained that a man was chasing her. The grocer called her home and the police

35

department. They picked up the man who, we later found out, had been in prison for rape.

Children should carry identification cards complete with their name, address, and phone number. If possible, their blood type and emergency numbers, such as the police department and grandparents' phone numbers, should be included. The card should be made out of a sturdy piece of cardboard with at least $1 in change taped to the back for emergency phone calls. Then it should be covered with a clear plastic wrap to help protect it from dirt and excess moisture. Children should carry their card with them at all times, preferably in a deep pocket so that it cannot be seen by anyone.

An alternative to a card is an identification disc or dog tag. These are available through Child Guard, which is sponsored by the American Federation of Police. For information write to Child Guard Data Center, 1100 NE 125th Street, North Miami, Florida 33161, or call (305) 891–1700.

Points to remember about names are the following:

- Names or name tags should not be on anything the child takes outside of his home except a concealed identification card.
- Warn children about the potential danger in carrying or wearing any articles with their name on them.
- Children should always carry an identification card or wear an identification disc or dog tag that is concealed by clothing.
- Children's clothing should be marked with proper identification that is concealed. If a child is abducted, and the clothing is found, such information could prove valuable to the police.

MEMORIZING IMPORTANT DATA

The child should memorize important information in the event that identification cards or tags are lost. Children with clear, bright minds should have no difficulty committing important phone numbers and addresses to memory. Teach them early in life that memorizing can be a happy experience, and they will respond positively.

If your child has difficulty memorizing, the following three games will be a fun and exciting way to accomplish teaching him or her important data. The games are progressive. Your child will learn skills that will help with each successive game.

The first and simplest game involves no words; it teaches observance skills. The second game teaches your child to associate words and pictures, committing them to memory. The third and last game deals directly with the vital information you want your child to memorize.

Small children who do not know how to write can be aided by parents or older siblings if the children wish to write a list of items for the first game. Or they may be permitted to tell you which items they recall.

GAME ONE

Materials needed: Small prizes, one pencil per child, four papers per child, one grocery bag, grocery items.

Groceries: round one

1. Place five food items inside a grocery bag, but do not allow the children to see the items.
2. Have the children sit in a circle on the floor.
3. Tell them that you will dump the items on the floor. They will have one minute to look at the items before you gather them into the sack.
4. Put the items back in the sack.
5. After the items are replaced in the sack, hand out pencils and paper. Ask the children to write the items on the paper as they recall them.
6. Collect the papers.
7. Award a small prize to the child who remembered the most.

Groceries: round two

1. Add five new items to the five old items in the grocery bag.
2. Dump the items onto the floor in the middle of the children's circle. Time one and a half minutes before you pick them up.
3. Pass out new paper and have the children recall and record the items.
4. Collect the papers.
5. Award a small prize to the winner of the second round.

Groceries: round three

1. Add five new items to the ten old ones in the sack.
2. Dump the items in the midst of the children and time two minutes before picking them up.
3. Pass out new paper.
4. After the children have recorded the items, collect their papers.
5. Award a prize to the winner of round three.

Groceries: round four

1. Add five new items to the fifteen old ones in the sack.
2. Dump the items in the midst of the children, and time three minutes before collecting them.
3. Pass out new paper.
4. After the children have reported their answers, collect their papers.
5. Award a special prize to the fourth round winner. Consolation prizes and praise can be offered to the other participants. Remember to reward the child who tries the hardest. The child who cannot write and must rely on memory should also receive acknowledgment.

GAME TWO

The Missing Song

Materials needed: Scissors, colored pencils or felt-tip markers, twelve-inch-long colored strips made from cardboard or poster board.

Directions:

1. Select an amusing song that your children do not know.
2. Prepare the foot-long strips cut from cardboard or poster board. You should have one colorful word strip for each sentence of the song.
3. Write the first sentence on a strip. The letters should be clear and easily read.

Write the second sentence on the second strip and so on until all the sentences have been prepared on strips. Colorfully drawn pictures can substitute for certain words. For example, instead of writing "I am a child who loves my dog" substitute a picture of an eye for the word *I,* and for the word *child* draw a picture of a child or a small stick figure. In place of the word *love* substitute the drawing of a heart. The word *dog* can be replaced by a drawing of the family dog. Your sentence will read as shown in the accompanying illustration.

Each strip should replace with drawings as many words as possible in the sentence for which it stands. This will add extra creativity and enjoyment to the game. Pictures are also much easier to remember than words.

4. Have the children sit in a semicircle. Position yourself in front of them. Hold up the first strip for them to use. Teach the children the words and tune to the first sentence.
5. Now hold up the second strip. Teach the children the tune and words of the second sentence.

6. Continue through the song in this manner until the children have learned all the strips and can sing the entire song with ease. Strips can be kept visible and together by pinning them to a large bulletin board.
7. Remove the first strip and challenge the children to sing the missing sentence.
8. When they have accomplished this task, remove the second strip. Challenge the children to sing it by heart.
9. Continue in this manner, strip by strip, until the entire song is missing. Challenge the children to sing the whole song by memory.
10. A prize can be awarded to the whole group for excellent participation.

The first two games are intended for children aged three to twelve years. The third game is primarily for four- to eight-year-old children.

GAME THREE

All About Me

Materials needed: Scissors, colored pencils, felt-tip markers, twelve-inch-long colored strips made from cardboard or poster board.

Directions:
1. Prepare three colorful strips. Remember to replace words with drawings.
2. Write each child's name on a strip. It should read: "My name is (child's name and picture)."
3. Write each child's complete address on a second strip. It should read: "My (drawing of house) is at (address)."
4. The last strip should read: "My (drawing of phone) number is (child's phone number)."

5. Work to help each child repeat the information on the strip. In the first week spend fifteen minutes a day working with each child until you are sure he or she can recall the information on the strips. During the next month, work on the strips twice a week. Allow each child to take his or her strips and keep them in an important place in the child's room where he or she can see them often. Reward each child's efforts and continue to reinforce the training by occasionally asking him or her to repeat all of the vital information.

Strips may be made for any extra information you want a child to learn, such as grandparents' phone numbers or the numbers of the police department. Phone Field Days will help to reinforce learning vital phone numbers.

TELEVISION AS A TEACHER

A great deal of controversy is brewing about the effects that television viewing has on children. Many parents want to see changes that will foster safety awareness for their families. A mother expresses her opinion as follows:

> *Even on toothpaste commercials they show kids running through town all the way home. They make you think it is safe for kids to run unaccompanied anywhere they want. What does that make kids think?*

A father shares his concern:

> *I've noticed that there are not many public service announcements about child abuse during prime time. I'd like to see that changed.*

A grandmother remarked that she wanted to visit her grandchildren, but they wouldn't give up Saturday morning cartoons, so she watched with them:

> *I wondered then if these precious children were thinking that if anything ever happened to them, they would have super powers to take care of themselves or that super heroes would fly down to their rescue.*

Even with television's imperfections, it can teach positive lessons that will be long remembered. There are excellent and educational safety programs to view. Through planning, instead of random selection, you as a parent can detour past less acceptable programming to use television as a teaching tool. This type of viewing can play an instrumental part in helping you to teach your child to be aware of the problems and dangers in the world. You must use discretion, however, when selecting safety programs to prevent alarming your child. It is unnecessary to use fear tactics in training children about safety. Be aware of the type of viewing that would frighten your child, and monitor such programs with care.

Television shows with such themes as child molestation, rape, and abduction are being shown increasingly. Excellent local documentaries can be instructive as to the types of dangers that the children in your community have encountered, such as sexual abuse, abduction, prostitution, drug addiction, and teenage pregnancy. You can support good programming by encouraging television coverage of such news. Few programs can have the long-term benefit that these presentations have.

A teacher tells the following story:

Jennifer is a first grader. Her parents are good friends of mine, and one day I was visiting them when a local station put on a documentary about child abduction in the area. Her mom had complained in the past because all Jenny would watch were cartoons. She didn't expect her to watch the program with us. Jenny sat down and seemed only mildly interested at first. Before long I noticed that she could not take her eyes off the television! She didn't seem afraid. Instead, she was really interested in the safety rules that were being taught.

Chapter 3

Parental Rights and Obligations

Parents have rights concerning their children that cannot be taken away except by the law. Yet with their rights come obligations and the never-ending challenge to care for and protect their young.

It seems inevitable that in our rushed society parents are sometimes shuffled around and treated as though they don't know what is best for their own children. In most instances, a concerned parent is capable of making decisions without tutoring. The nurse who tells parents to leave their child alone in a hospital or a nursery school teacher who insists that they stay away during certain hours may mean well. However, the ultimate right to make a decision on such commonplace matters lies with the parents. Considering institutional rules and legal rights and obligations to assure their children's safety, parents can strike a harmonious balance.

- Parents have the right and the obligation to be protective of and caring for their children.
- Parents have a right and obligation to provide education and safety training for their children.
- Parents have an obligation to discipline with love in order to teach important principles.

- Parents have an obligation to inform their children of the dangers they may encounter without causing fearfulness or insecurity in the child.

- Parents have an obligation to repeat the safety-training test every two years and reinforce safety principles on a daily basis for their child's continued protection.

- Parents have the right to know their children's peers, teachers, or anyone involved in any aspect of their children's lives.

- Parents have the right and obligation to know where their children are.

- Parents have a right to insist that schools, hospitals, and other institutions use care in treating children and their families respectfully. If a parent wishes to check on a child, she or he should be welcomed to do so.

- Parents have an obligation to understand their children and a right to know what happens in their everyday lives.

- Guardians are ultimately responsible to the child for the conditions in which they place the child.

- Parents have the obligation to abide by safety rules in order to reinforce training for their children.

ENTERING YOUR CHILD'S WORLD

When parents want to teach safety, draw out children's fears, or develop more unified family relationships, they need to enter the young child's world through play. Children grow physically and mentally through play. It is their work and the avenue through which they begin to perceive their world.

The following is a demonstration of a mother playing puppets with her four-year-old child to bring out feelings that her daughter may never have intended to share:

Mother: (working turtle puppet) Hi! Isn't this a pretty day?
Jessica: (working monkey puppet) Yes.
Mother: I've been thinking about my best friend. Are you my best friend?

Jessica: I don't know.
Mother: My best friend is my mom.
Jessica: Why is it your mommie?
Mother: Because she listens to me and helps me. She feeds me and teaches me all the things I need to know, so that I can grow up safely.
Jessica: My mommie does, too!
Mother: I have another best friend.
Jessica: Who?
Mother: My dad. He loves me lots, too. Who is your best friend, number one and two?
Jessica: My mommie is one and my daddy is two.
Mother: (turtle still speaking) How come?
Jessica: Because they love me, silly!
Mother: Do they teach you safety?
Jessica: Yes, I can't go across the street alone.
Mother: What else?
Jessica: Not to talk to a stranger.
Mother: Tell me more! (turtle puppet jumps up and down as if excited)
Jessica: Not to get in anyone's car and go away.
Mother: Did your parents tell you there is a right way and a wrong way to be touched?
Jessica: No.
Mother: It's true! Your mommie and daddy love you. They touch you to bathe you and dress you.
Jessica: And put medicine on my cuts.
Mother: Yes. Those are good ways to be touched. Do you ever go to the doctor?
Jessica: Yes.
Mother: Does he touch you?
Jessica: Yes.
Mother: Why?
Jessica: To get me well.
Mother: Is that a good way to be touched?
Jessica: Yes, it gets me well, silly!

Mother: When your mommie and daddy and the doctor touch you, they do it to help you.

Jessica: I know that.

Mother: But there are people who might touch you to hurt you.

Jessica: (No response)

Mother: If anyone ever touched your private body parts, other than your mom or dad, would you tell them about it?

Jessica: I don't know.

Mother: Do your parents want to help you and take care of you?

Jessica: Yes.

Mother: Then would you tell them if someone touched your private body parts?

Jessica: Can they help me if I do?

Mother: Yes, your mommie and daddy are always here to help you.

Jessica: Then I'd tell them.

Mother: That's the right thing to do. You are a very good girl to do the right thing.

Jessica: I know.

Mother: What if someone touched you and told you to keep it a secret from your parents?

Jessica: I'd tell them, silly turtle!

Mother: Let's say that person told you they would hurt you more, then what would you do?

Jessica: I'd tell my mom.

Mother: That's good. Would your parents believe you?

Jessica: (No response)

Mother: Do they believe you most of the time?

Jessica: Yes.

Mother: Then would they believe you now?

Jessica: Yes. I would tell them.

Mother: That's the right thing to do, isn't it?

Jessica: Yes. Now let me ask the questions!

Children may change the subject, and if this happens parents can redirect it if desired. The following is an example of a child's changing the subject from safety and a parent's redirecting the conversation. This time a father plays dolls with his daughter, Shelley.

Father: (using a large doll) Hi! Can you tell me how to get to Upton Street? I am lost.

Shelley: (using small doll) It's over there.

Father: Where?

Shelley: Over that way!

Father: I'll never find it. Listen, I could sure use your help. Can you come with me to show me?

Shelley: Daddy, let's play with my Barbie.

Father: Well, O.K., Barbie can play. Do you think she would be a good mommie?

Shelley: Yes! She can be the mommie.

Father: Let's play like she is in the house and you are still outside.

Shelley: No! I want her to be outside, too.

Father: O.K. Can she garden?

Shelley: She can do everything, Daddy!

Father: Then let's let her be in the garden, and the Shelley doll and stranger can be in the front yard.

Shelley: O.K.

Father: Now, little girl, I sure need your help. Can you come with me so that I can find Upton Street?

Shelley: No. My daddy won't let me go with strangers!

The father has successfully redirected the conversation back to safety. Now he must stop the game and give Shelley an evaluation of her doll's actions. He must use care to criticize the doll— not Shelley. He should remember also to offer praise when it is appropriate.

Father: Shelley, do you know what?

Shelley: What, Daddy?

Father: I'm really glad that you feel that Mommie can do everything. That would make your mommie very happy. But I feel worried about your doll.

Shelley: Why, Daddy? She's O.K.

Father: I feel worried because she talked to the stranger.

Shelley: What's wrong with that?

Father: Well, can you tell the difference between a good person and a bad person?

Shelley: I don't know.

Father: That's right. You don't know because it's hard to tell the difference between someone who is good and someone who is bad.

Shelley: Then what should she do?

Father: Well, I'd like to see her turn around and run and scream for her mother.

Shelley: Is that what you want me to do, too?

Father: If a stranger ever asks for your help, that's what I want you to do. Do you know what? I'm proud of you for learning this lesson.

Shelley: Let's play more! I'll be the stranger, and you be the little girl.

Role reversals can be beneficial in play and should be allowed. During play periods parents can introduce the "stranger game" and incorporate molesters' tactics into the play. Refer to the TV news, newspapers, and magazine articles to remain updated on current tactics. These can be incorporated into play.

Puppet and doll play can be an advantageous tool when used properly. Consider the following points for play activities:

- Use puppets, dolls, and stuffed animals to play the part of friend, stranger, and child.

- Outline a list of safety techniques that you want to teach your child. Outline a second list of techniques that child abductors and/or molesters use.

- Use female dolls and grandma and grandpa dolls in the role of a stranger or a friend who molests.

- Let playtime include safety topics, such as children's personal rights, answering the door and phone, and keeping secrets.

- Allow children to express their fears and concerns freely.

- Grandparents can teach important safety topics through discussion and play. They should be included in safety training if they live near your family.

- Use your child's real-life situation to structure safety training through play. If your child has a visible handicap, let him or her learn to handle play situations using a doll with the same handicap. Patiently instruct the child through play about the safety precautions you want used.

- Molested children can respond positively to play therapy. Parents may rely on authorities in the field of child sexual abuse to guide them in learning the best play techniques.

- Mentally retarded children can respond well to play techniques that teach important concepts. Patient parents can effectively use playtime to teach basic safety principles to the mentally retarded child, but the amount of teaching that can be accomplished depends on the severity of the child's handicap. These children are especially vulnerable to the child molester, and every effort to protect and train them should be made. Use the tools (art work, dolls, stuffed animals, etc.) to which they respond well in order to teach valuable safety concepts.

- Learn to listen to your child's input during playtime. You can build on what the child already knows and teach what he or she does not know.

- Teach your child danger signals. Explain that a danger signal is a sign that alerts the child that there is something wrong. Parents may work with children to expand this list:
  - If an adult asks your child for help, it is a danger signal.
  - If an adult tells your child to keep a secret, it is a danger signal.
  - If an adult other than a relative takes your child's picture without your permission, it is a danger signal.
  - If in person or on the telephone an adult tries to get information from your child, it is a danger signal.
  - If an adult approaches your child and wants to take her or him somewhere, it is a danger signal.
  - If an adult in authority over your child tries to overrule the child's personal rights, it is a danger signal.

Children are a precious resource, supposedly safe under the bright canopy of a free society that extends its protective power over them. Yet, within the freedoms we enjoy are the impenetrable black holes left by our laws or the lack of them. Out of this vacuum of darkness come the child molester, kidnapper, rapist, and murderer. Such offenders damage the future of our country each time they lay hands on a child.

It is up to parents to reverse the trend. Safety training cannot be left in the hands of others. It is an act of love that begins at home. Each parent is ultimately responsible to his or her child for the way that child is trained and protected. The test in Part Two will be a valuable aid in helping you to begin this training process.

PART TWO

BEING PREPARED: TESTS AND GAMES

Chapter 4

The Written/Oral Safety Test

The purpose of the written/oral and safety skills test is much like that of the home fire drill. It is required to inform, give detailed experience, and train the child before trouble occurs.

The two-part quiz includes written and skills tests. The written part may be given as an oral test for children too young to read. The quiz should be given in a relaxed family environment, such as a special evening when the family is gathered around.

Reassure each child that there is no failing grade and that she or he will have the opportunity to learn all the information on the test. If the child tires before the test is completed, plan another evening to finish.

Explain to your child that this is not a school test. It is given out of love and concern for him. The exam will train the child to be responsible for part of his or her own care.

Give the test to your child as soon as the child is capable of understanding the difference between safety and danger, preferably by age four. Accordingly, children aged four to sixteen should take the test. Older teens may review it if desired.

The test invites discussion and after grading should be thoroughly reviewed, question by question. The child should have a working solution to each problem and a correct answer to every question. You should remain patient and listen respectfully to each child's opinions and answers. You may add questions to the test if they are pertinent to the child's safety environment because home situations may differ greatly from family to family.

An *answer review* to explain questions is included for you to add to the discussion. Extra situations are added at the end of the test. You may discuss these special situations at the end of the test or on some other occasion. But you should discuss them before the skills test is given. Instructions for the skills test follow the written/oral exam.

PREPARATORY IDEAS

Special family nights involve several important factors that enrich the child's learning environment:

- In preparation for the test, designate one evening each week as family training night. Without fail, set aside the evening as a special time when each family member is expected to be present. Try to use the same time each week. The written/oral test can be easily implemented during special family training night.

- The meeting can begin as soon after the evening meal as possible. The time must not conflict with the bedtime of small children. Some families may prefer to select a time on Saturday instead of a weekday evening.

- The setting should be relaxed and free from interruption. Telephones may be unplugged or left unanswered. However, it may be preferable to assign an older family member to handle phone calls and visitors during this time so that the family night may be free from disturbance. The television should be turned off, and in its place relaxing music may be played as the family gathers together.

FAMILY INVOLVEMENT

The entire family should contribute to the planning of the special training evening. In this way, each member will feel needed and take his or her responsibility more seriously.

Family participation is necessary to add creativity and order to the evening. It is important to involve all family members in the assignments in order to create a positive learning atmosphere. Even young children will enjoy the assignments if they are promoted in a pleasurable way. The family circle chore charts (see pp. 55, 56) will designate preparation chores for each family member. Call the participating individuals together for a brief brainstorming session, and write a list of preparations that will be necessary. Each family's list will differ because of their own priorities. One family may write a list that involves cleaning the room to be used for family training night. Another may wish to prepare refreshments and add an activity such as a game or skit. Still another may wish to begin the evening with a brief prayer. *The Family Home Evening Resource Book* of the Church of Jesus Christ of Latter-Day Saints suggests that families use a chart to organize special family night activities. Keep your list of activities in mind as you make the family chore chart.

- A family of four or more should obtain a piece of sturdy cardboard approximately eighteen by eighteen inches.
- The board may be covered with colorful wallpaper or Contact paper.
- Make a light pencil outline of a circle approximately ten inches in diameter.
- Outside the borders of the circle, write the chores to be performed in bold, black letters.
- Cut the premeasured circle out of a heavy piece of brightly colored poster board. The names of each participating family member should be written in corresponding black letters on the circle.
- Attach the circle to the square board by a prong fastener to allow for easy rotation.

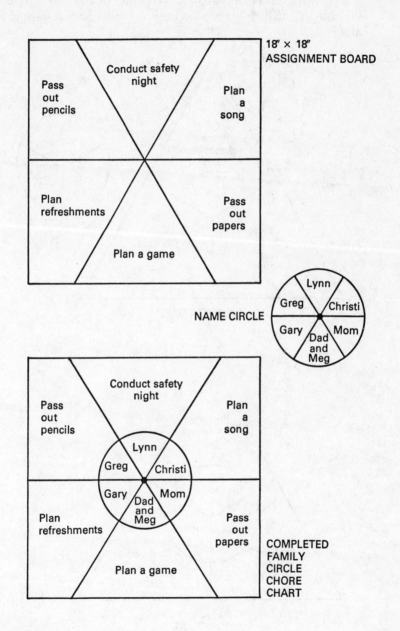

18″ × 18″
ASSIGNMENT BOARD

Pass out pencils

Conduct safety night

Plan a song

Plan refreshments

Plan a game

Pass out papers

NAME CIRCLE

Lynn
Greg
Christi
Gary
Dad and Meg
Mom

Pass out pencils

Conduct safety night

Plan a song

Lynn
Greg
Christi
Gary
Dad and Meg
Mom

Plan refreshments

Plan a game

Pass out papers

COMPLETED FAMILY CIRCLE CHORE CHART

- It is permissible to write two names together on the name circle in the case of small children who cannot fulfill chore assignments alone.

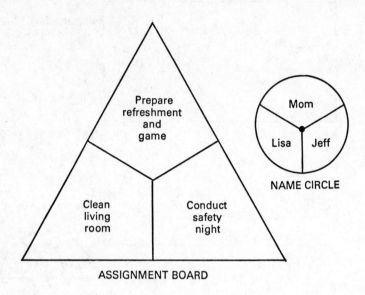

ASSIGNMENT BOARD

NAME CIRCLE

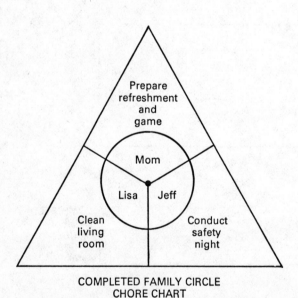

COMPLETED FAMILY CIRCLE
CHORE CHART

The circle chore chart is an assignment board that can be made for any size family to fit its particular needs. The accompanying illustration is an example of a circle chore chart for two parents and five children.

For a family of three a triangle may be drawn and cut from sturdy cardboard. The sides should each measure twelve inches in length and the bottom should measure nine and a half inches across. The board may be covered in a colorful paper with chore assignments written on it in large black letters. A three-and-a-half-inch name circle may be cut and attached to the middle of the triangle with a prong fastener. Remember to draw the outline of the name circle before writing chore assignments on the chart. The accompanying illustration is an example of a chore chart for three.

Chapter 5

Preparation Games and the Written/Oral Safety Test

THE CHORE SACK

The chore sack is another way to add zest and fun to assignments that must be done in preparation for the test on family training night. Your list of assignments may include making refreshments, vacuuming or sweeping the room to be used, preparing an activity (e.g., a game or skit), preparing a song, and giving a prayer.

Place the following items in the chore sack to indicate an assignment: a cook's hat labeled "Refreshments," a small car broom labeled "Clean Room," a colorful piece of a puzzle or game to be labeled "Game or Skit," a small songbook or a piece of colorful construction paper in the form of a musical note labeled with the word "Song." A small Bible may be labeled "Prayer." The day before family night blindfold the children, turn them in a circle three times, and have them pull an object from the sack. They will be responsible for fulfilling the assignment connected with the object.

In *The Family Home Evening Resource Book,* the Church of Jesus Christ of Latter-Day Saints suggests a balloon game. The game is also appropriate for family night preparations for the test. Write the assignments on small pieces of paper and put each of them inside a balloon. Blow up the balloons and place them in a room. Each child can choose the balloon he or she desires and pop it. The child will then be responsible for the assignment found in the popped balloon.

PARENT'S PLANNING TIME

Because the purpose of the special family training night is to offer the safety test, it is imperative that parents sit down together to plan the test schedule.

For the first family training night, plan to cover written test questions one through fifteen and the answers that are provided as guidelines. The second family training night should include questions fifteen through thirty with the answers. The third week covers the remaining twenty questions. In the fourth week, study and discuss the situation at the end of the written test. Add any safety information that you believe is pertinent to your children's needs.

The skills test should begin the week following the completion of the written test. Skills are divided into three stages of performance, with the first stage being the easiest to master. Stage I basic skills should not require more than two weeks to complete. The estimated completion time for Stage II intermediate skills is three to four weeks. Stage III advanced skills will require approximately three to four weeks to complete.

The preparation agenda for a family might read:

Tuesday family training night assignments
- Dad: conducts meeting
- Mom: prepares refreshments
- Richard: cleans living room
- Bill: selects opening song
- Rick: gives prayer and assists with refreshments
- Jan: conducts safety skit

Approx. times required	Training night activity
15 minutes—7:00–7:15	Dad: welcomes family, briefly describes evening plans.
	Rick: gives prayer.
	Bill: leads song.
	Jan: conducts safety skit (5 minutes).
25 minutes—7:15–7:40	Test time: questions one through fifteen.
20 minutes—7:40–8:00	Discussion and answer review.
8:00	End meeting. Refreshments.

The number of children involved in the test and the family schedule will ultimately determine the time needed to complete the test for each family. If the schedule is strictly adhered to, the minimal time for both tests will run twelve to fourteen weeks. Keep in mind that it is allowable to cover the entire written test in one night if you wish. Your family may also complete the skills tests more quickly, but take care not to omit any skills.

If your family is large and includes children from preschool to teenagers, the test may be given by age groups. Begin with four- to ten-year-olds, who are usually more vulnerable because of their lack of knowledge. Then test ten- to sixteen-year-olds.

The entire test period is one in which enthusiasm must be generated for the cause of safety. It is a time to gather young ones near, encouraging some discussion of the subject each day. Our children view the world with a spellbound sense of wonder, which makes their early years an opportune time for safety training.

Ezra Taft Benson, one of the presidents of the Church of Jesus Christ of Latter-Day Saints, once counseled parents in this way:

Encourage your children to come to you for counsel with their problems and questions by listening to them every day. Discuss with them such important matters as dating, sex and other matters affecting their growth and development, and do it early enough so they will not obtain information from questionable sources.

This simple wisdom is often overlooked as we strive to give our children the material benefits of life. It is our time, not the luxuries of life, that will influence their thinking and ability to deal with the difficulties they may one day face. If we neglect to offer them our time and praise, little else can make up the difference.

The value of praise in any type of teaching should be highly acclaimed. The repetition of safety ideas coupled with direct praise for a job well done can teach lessons and possibly save lives.

A young mother relates the following story about her son and daughter:

We taught our kids about safety in family home evenings, and it has paid off since! They were walking home from school when a pickup truck stopped on the other side of the road. A man in a ski hat got out of the truck and motioned for them to come to him. Because of what they had been taught, they ran across an open field and went to a friend's home to call me. After it happened, I let them know I was real proud of them for listening. It saved their lives. I taught them to always go in two's and never to talk to anyone who approaches them, and if there is a way, to try and get as much description as possible but not to endanger themselves. We don't play mysterious games with our kids. We tell them what these people do to children. As I said, it pays!

Written/oral safety test

For questions 1 through 8 circle "yes" or "no."

1. Can you trust everyone?
   Yes   No

2. Do you *always* know whom to trust?
   Yes   No

3. Can you *always* trust your neighbors?
   Yes   No

4. Can you *always* trust your parent's friends?
   Yes   No

5. Can you *always* trust your friends?
   Yes   No

6. Can you *always* trust strangers?
   Yes   No

7. Can you *always* trust your teachers?
   Yes   No

8. Can you *always* trust most people?
   Yes   No

9. What are your personal rights?

10. Would you tell your parents if someone *asks* to take your picture or if someone *takes* your picture? Why?

11. Do you believe that adults should ask only adults for help? Why? If an adult asks for your help, would you:
    a. Help the adult find his or her dog?
    b. Help the adult locate an address?
    c. Help the adult find a friend?
    d. Help the adult who says he or she is lost?
    e. Take candy, food, money, drinks, or gifts if he or she offers them?
    f. Help the adult in any way?

12. Should you walk near a car when someone is in it?

13. Would you get into a car without the permission of your parents?

14. What is a distress word? How would you use it?

15. Someone asks you to touch his or her private body parts and insists you obey. The person tells you not to tell your parents. What would you do?

16. Do you think you can protect yourself?

17. If an adult asks you to keep a secret from your parents, what should you do?

18. Would you accept money, gifts, or anything else from someone outside the family? Would you tell your parents if you were offered anything from someone outside your family?

19. Would you go into anyone's home without a parent's permission?

20. You are away from home and feel frightened and want to talk to your parents. Do you have a personal right to use the phone?

21. Do you know how to use different types of phones?
    a. Dial pay phone, punch button pay phone.
    b. Dial home phone, punch button home phone.

22. A man or woman talks a lot to you about sex or love and tries to touch your private body parts. He or she tells you it's all right and not to tell your parents but to keep it part of your secret game. What would you do?

23. If you are at home alone and someone knocks on the door, what would you do?

24. If the telephone rings and you are alone, would you tell the caller that you are alone? If the caller asks for your parents and they are not at home, what would you say?

25. A doctor, policeman, minister, or anyone touches your private body parts and tells you to keep it a secret. You are told to obey or you will be put in jail or hurt. What would you do?

26. If you are molested by someone, do you believe your parents will still love and help you? Will they protect you from its happening again?

27. Your parents leave you with a babysitter and tell you to mind him or her. But the babysitter starts acting strange and wants to touch you or hurt you. The babysitter says if you do what she says, she will buy you anything you want. What should you do?

28. Would you yell loud if someone tried to hurt you or take you away? How loud? Would you bite or kick?

29. Should you wear your name on any of your clothes or have your name on belongings you take outside your home? Why?

30. If you don't want to be with someone, would you tell your parents why?

31. An uncle or other relative tries to touch your private body parts. He says your mother told you to mind him and she'll be mad if you don't. What would you do? Does a relative have a right to touch your private body parts or hurt you?

32. When you are afraid or lonely, can you talk to your parents about it?

33. Your parents' best friend is _____. If _____ tried to touch or hurt you, what would you do?

34. You are playing on the playground at school and notice a person watching you from a car *or* from on foot. What would you do?

35. You are playing in the yard and see someone driving slowly around your neighborhood. What would you do?

36. You are selling candy or cookies for a scout project, and you must go door to door. What would you do if:
    a. Someone invites you inside?
    b. Someone exposes his or her body to you?
    c. Someone says he or she will give you candy if you will do something for that person?

37. Your parents are not at home. Should you keep your dog inside the house if he is housetrained and your parents approve? Why?

38. Your parents work, and you must come home alone. When you put the key in the door, you notice that it is already opened. What should you do?

39. There is a drug problem at your school. One of your friends offers you pills, a powder, candy, or a drink. What would you do?

40. Your teacher tells you to stay after school. He tells you that you will flunk the class if you don't do what he wants. He wants you to touch him and then let him touch you. Then he threatens you and tells you not to tell anyone. What would you do?

41. You have been molested and tell your parents what has happened, but they are busy. They act as though they aren't listening. You are not sure if they believe you. Will you try to tell someone else, or will you try to forget about what happened and not mention it again?

42. Should you tell your parents where you are going if you want to leave home for any reason?

43. Do you carry a wallet or card with your name, address, phone number, and money in it? Should you? Why? Or why not?

44. Do you think you need to follow safety rules?

45. Who is a stranger? Would you ever ride with a stranger? Would you ride with someone you know even if your parents advise you not to?

46. If someone tried to pick you up or get you into his or her car, what would you do?

47. Do you know emergency phone numbers and how to dial them? What are they?

48. You are in a store with your grandparents. They are busy, and you see a dog outside that you want to pet. What would you do?

49. When you are out with your parents (to a movie, restaurant, or store), should you stay close to them, or is it all right to wander a little? Should you go to a public bathroom alone, or should you ask a parent to go with you? If you get lost should you ask the person behind the counter for help or someone who is wandering around?

50. Should you ever walk anyplace alone? Should you stay in a car by yourself or with other children?

SITUATIONS FOR DISCUSSION

You have a special adult friend who likes you very much. You like this person very much, too. You and your friend talk about a lot of things, and he or she buys you special gifts. Then one day your friend asks you to take off your clothes and says he or she wants to touch you. You don't like this idea because your parents have told you that this is wrong. You say "no" very firmly, but your friend says he or she won't like you anymore if you don't do what is asked of you.

- What is the danger signal that warns you something is wrong?
- Has your friend asked you to do something wrong and even dangerous?
- How would you feel if your friend didn't like you anymore?
- Is this person really your friend?
- What would you do if this happened to you?

A neighbor you know touches or hurts you. You are going to tell your parents. The neighbor says your parents won't believe you because you are just a kid and grownups believe only other grownups. He or she says that you are a tattletale and that he or she will tell your parents you're lying.

- Do grownups believe only grownups?

- When people call you names like "tattletale," does it bother you? Why?
- Are you afraid for people to tell your parents you are lying even when you are not lying?
- Will your parents believe others before they believe you? Do you trust your parents?

The janitor at school asks you to stay after the other kids leave. He wants you to help him move some chairs. You feel worried about his request because he always does this work himself. You want to run. But you are afraid you'll look like a sissy.

- Is it all right to be afraid?
- Is it all right to express your feeling of fear?
- Is it more important to show people you are brave, or to be safe?
- Is there a danger signal in this situation? If so, what is it?
- What would you do if this happened to you?

You are at a scout meeting. All the scouts are busy working on their projects. You have already finished and decide to leave. You don't tell anyone you are going because you plan to buy candy at the store and your parents would be angry if they found out.

- Have you done something dangerous?
- If so, what was it?
- Why was it dangerous?
- What is the right way to solve this problem?

You are playing ball in your yard. You see someone drop a kitten from a car across the road. You leave the yard to get to the kitten.

- Have you done something dangerous?
- If so, what have you done that is dangerous?
- Why is it dangerous?
- What is the safe way to solve this problem?

You are playing at a friend's home, inside her yard. A van pulls near the curb, and a nice-looking lady gets out. She asks you if you would like to help her by giving a home to one of her puppies. You can hear a puppy inside the van.

- What would you do?
- Do you believe this nice lady is a stranger?
- Do you believe you can trust her because you hear a puppy inside the van?
- Why could this situation be dangerous?
- What is the danger signal in this situation?

You have a new Sunday School teacher. He is a lot of fun, and all the kids love him. Sometimes he dresses in costumes and brings games to class. He can do lots of magic tricks. One day after class he asks you to go to the cleaning closet and promises to show you a great trick.

- What is the danger signal?
- What would you do?
- Has your Sunday School teacher asked you to do something wrong?
- Do you trust him because all the kids like him?
- What could happen if you go with him?

A policeman approaches you as you ride your bike to a friend's house. He says the police department is awarding free tickets for a famous rock star's concert to children who obey bicycle safety rules. He tells you that you have won two tickets but must go with him to the police station for the award. He says that you can call your parents and tell them about the tickets as soon as you arrive at the station. You really like the rock star and want to go to the concert.

- What would you do?
- Do you believe he is a policeman? Why?

- Can you always trust people who wear uniforms?
- If he showed you his badge, would you believe he was a policeman?
- Would it be dangerous to go with him? Why?
- What is the danger signal?

School is over, and you are waiting in the usual place for your mother to pick you up. A lady and man stop their car nearby. The lady walks toward you. She tells you that your mother went to the hospital because she was hurt in an accident. The lady promises to take you to your mother and tells you to hurry. You are afraid and worried about your family.

- What is the danger signal?
- What would you do?
- Can you trust a stranger who says there is an emergency?
- Would your mother call to tell you if someone else was picking you up from school?
- What would your parents want you to do?

You are in a store and steal a piece of candy. A teenaged boy tells you that he saw you take the candy. He says that he will tell the store manager and that you will be put in jail if you don't come with him.

- What is the danger signal?
- What would you do?
- Which is the best solution: to go with the young man and not get in trouble with the store? Or to stay in the store, ask for help, and admit that you took the candy?
- Why would it be dangerous to go with the young man?
- Is it better to admit you did something wrong and be safe or to try to hide a wrongdoing and be unsafe?

Your parents leave you at your grandfather's home while they go out to dinner. Your grandfather asks for a hug and wants you to sit on his lap. He unzips your pants and touches your private body parts. You know that this is wrong and ask him to stop. Then he promises to buy you the new bicycle that you have wanted for a long time if you will let him touch you. He asks you not to tell your parents that he has touched you.

- What is the danger signal?
- What would you do?
- Is it wrong for a relative to touch you in this way?
- Is it better to get a new bicycle and let your grandfather touch you or to tell your parents what happened?
- Why is it dangerous to let someone touch you in this way?

You are a student in a gymnastics class and have decided that you want to work hard so that you can compete in the Olympics someday. Your gym teacher tells you to do what he asks and you will be able to try out for the Olympics team. He says he will need to take your picture a lot of times. He promises to set up interviews with the Olympics authorities for you. Then he asks you to keep it a secret from everyone.

- What would you do?
- Does your gym teacher's promise seem strange in any way?
- Would you keep a secret from your parents?
- Why could this situation be dangerous?
- What is the danger signal?

Parents' Discussion Guide to Written/Oral Test

Question 1.   It is healthy for a child to trust people. The child's trust toward others indicates a good sense of security, which is vital for normal growth and development. Unfortunately, a child *cannot* and *should not* trust everyone. Be sure to explain the difference between good and bad people. Emphasize that everyone has a choice. Some people choose to do good things. Some choose to do bad things and hurt others. Bad people cannot be trusted. A child cannot tell the difference between good and bad people and must therefore be cautious about everyone.

Question 2. No one always knows whom to trust. Too often we make hasty judgments about who is trustworthy, and the mistake can be costly. Discuss making careful character judgments.

Question 3. Neighbors can be guilty of sexual misconduct with children. Don't establish fearfulness in your child's mind concerning neighbors, but help the child to be aware that neighbors, as well as others, can make the wrong choices and hurt children. Encourage your child to use caution around neighbors.

Question 4. Certainly we prefer to think that our friends can be trusted with our children. No parent would intentionally choose friends who would harm his or her children. Be prepared to put your feelings on the line, however, and tell your children that friends are just people. Not all people should be trusted.

Question 5. A child naturally trusts his friends and almost never questions a friend's motives. The older a child becomes, the more natural it will be for him or her to defend friends. Sometimes even a hint of parental disapproval will drive a child into an angry state, so use great care and judgment when approaching this subject. Explain that even friends can be involved with drugs or with people who harm children. Children must sometimes question their friends about what they are doing and why.

Question 6. We prefer to think that only strangers harm children. Strangers are among those who act criminally toward youngsters. Don't forget to emphasize, though, that strangers can help children as well as hurt them. Be sure that children understand that both men and women can be guilty of sexual abuse and kidnapping and that they must use caution around *any* stranger, regardless of how nice the person appears to be.

Question 7. We wrongfully assume that all teachers are loving and protective toward children. In fact, they are not *always* trustworthy any more than most other people. Coaches, teachers, and volunteers for children's organizations have been accused of sexual crimes against children. Discuss a teacher's role in your child's life.

Encourage your child to talk about each of his or her teachers and what the child likes and dislikes about them.

Question 8. Obviously not all people can be trusted. So it becomes necessary to use caution and teach children that we cannot *always* trust most people. Safety rules should be used at all times. Children and parents should discuss watching for danger signals around strangers, family, and friends. Emphasize that there are more good adults in the world than bad ones. But because children cannot tell the difference, they must use caution around all adults.

Question 9. Every child should be taught that he has personal rights that should be respected by all adults. Parents may add more rights to the basic list as they discuss the question with their children.

- I have a right to say no if someone touches or wants to touch the private parts of my body.
- I have the right to scream for help, even if I am told by a molester to be quiet and obey. I can obey my parents, but I don't have to obey someone who hurts me or wants to hurt me.
- I have the right to tell my parents everything that happens to me. They will always love me no matter what happens. If someone touches or hurts me and tells me to keep it a secret, I will still tell my parents because I have a right to their help.
- I have the right to use the phone to call home at any time when I want to talk to my parents.
- I have the right to have food, shelter, and clothing.
- I have the right to medical care.

- I have the right to be loved and cared for.
- I have the right to be educated.

Question 10. You must teach children that there is a difference between harmless and harmful picture taking. Family photographs and school pictures are not used to a child's disadvantage. Individuals involved in pornography, however, will use seemingly harmless excuses to take a child's picture. They may continue to make contact with the child after the first photo session. If this has happened to your child, get a complete description of the circumstances and individuals involved. Then contact the police. Keep the information in the child's personal file folder. Refer to Chapter 7. Continue your discussion, and read "The Wrong Kind of Picture Taking" in Chapter 2.

Question 11. Child sexual molesters are very cunning in appealing to a child's sense of sympathy, greed, or desires. Explain to your child the danger of helping any adult. Make certain that the child understands that adults don't need children's help because they are quite capable of helping themselves or asking other adults for help. Give suggestions to your child on what you want him or her to do if approached for help by an adult.

Question 12. Children should be warned to avoid parked cars with one or more adults inside. You can teach them to walk on the opposite side of the street and not to walk alone unless necessary. Discuss the dangers involved in walking near parked cars and the child's ability to protect himself.

Question 13. Discuss the obvious dangers of your child's getting into someone's car without your permission. Tell your child that if you have not given your permission, you will not know where he or she is and what is happening. The child also should not accept rides with friends, parents' friends, or other family members without parental consent.

Question 14. Children should be aware that adults are capable of telling lies to lure children away from parents. If a child is confronted with this situation, he or she should immediately get away from the person involved, seek help, and look for a phone to call home. Inform your child personally of all changes you make in transporting the child where he or she must go. The child should not talk to anyone who is trying to lure him or her away, but if a conversation does ensue, the child should ask for a distress word.

Question 15. Explain that "someone" could be a friend, family member, or stranger. In any case, tell your child what you expect him or her to do and why. Express concern for your child's well-being in your discussion.

Question 16. Many children believe they are capable of protecting themselves from anyone who would harm them. This is especially true of boys. If your child believes he is capable of self-protection, it is wise to prove to him physically that he is not as strong as he thinks. Games such as Indian wrestling will convince most children of their weakness in comparison to adults. If your child is sure he could outrun an attacker, prove by racing him that he cannot. It is important not to create insecurity or make your child feel extremely vulnerable, so use care in your attempts. The point is to sufficiently prove a child's weakness and discourage him from taking foolish chances.

Question 17. Explain to your child that you love him and want to be involved in everything that happens to him. This is your job as a parent. Secrets can be dangerous, and you don't want your child to keep any secrets because it could prove dangerous to his or her well-being. Be sure your child understands that adults have no right to ask children to keep secrets from their parents. Refer to Chapter 2, "Teach Your Children Not to Keep Secrets."

Question 18. Explain the possible danger of accepting gifts or money from people outside the family, except on special occasions when friends offer them. Refer to "A Pet for Paula—A Gift of Coins" in Chapter 2.

Question 19. Explain the dangers of a child entering someone's home without permission. The dangers include the following:

- No one would know where to look for the child.
- Another person could hurt the child without fear of discovery.
- Parents and friends would be worried.
- Possible sexual abuse and even death for the child could occur.

Question 20. One of a child's rights is to call parents at any time. Notify relatives, friends' parents, and schools to allow the child to call home if he or she becomes frightened. It is your right as a parent to expect others to cooperate with your wishes, but explain to your children that they must not take advantage of this right.

Question 21. As stated in the previous question, the child *always* has a right to use a phone. If your child does not know how to use different types of phones, plan a time in the near future to teach the procedure. Refer to "Teach Your Child to Use the Telephone" in Chapter 1.

Question 22. It is to be hoped that your child will respond that she or he would tell you if a stranger were to molest or bother the child in any way. Encourage this response.

Question 23. Police advise that a child at home alone should not answer the door because an intruder could harm the child. Be sure that your child knows to answer the door only when an adult family member is present. The child may allow people to come in only with parental permission. Refer to "When Your Child Answers the Door" in Chapter 1.

Question 24. Instruct your child never to tell a caller that he or she is alone. Tell your child that callers can try to break into homes and harm children. If a caller should ask for a child's parents when they are away from home, the child should reply, "My parents can't come to the phone right now. I'll take a message and have them call you in a few minutes." Refer to "When Your Child Answers the Phone" in Chapter 1.

Question 25. Explain that even persons in positions of authority can harm children. Tell the child never to be afraid of anyone's threat but to report any incident immediately to you.

Question 26. This question should give the child time to evaluate your relationship with her. Explain that you will always love and help her no matter what happens to her. You are her most trustworthy friend and will keep the offender from harming her again.

Question 27. Explain to your child that even babysitters can be guilty of crimes against children. If the babysitter begins to act strangely or harm the child, the child must run for help. Make an arrangement with a responsible mother in a neighborhood home to whom the child may turn for help. The child should explain the situation to the neighbor and ask to use the phone to call the police. Tell the child the danger of accepting bribes and that you will reward him for doing the right thing. And remember when you are out to call home several times to check on your child. Instruct your child to use the distress word if he or she is in trouble.

Question 28. This question gives you an opportunity to test your child's lung power. Work with the child to develop a very loud scream, and encourage her or him to kick and bite anyone who threatens his or her safety. If possible enroll your child in a self-defense course for children that is offered by a qualified instructor.

Question 29. Refer to and read the section on personal identification in Chapter 2.

Question 30. Encourage your children to talk to you on a daily basis. Make a special effort to tell your child each day of your love. If there is someone the child dislikes, explain that you want to know why. Knowing this information could protect the child someday.

Question 31. Encourage your child to tell any sexual offender "No!" in clear, convincing terms. Practice this with your child. Say that no one, even a relative, has a right to put his or her hands on a child in any harmful or sexual way. Assure your child that no matter what anyone says, you will not be angry with him or her for telling an offender "no." It is not a matter of obedience but a matter of rights and safety for the child.

Question 32. Apologize for times when you have failed to listen, and promise to make an effort to improve if necessary. Encourage your child to talk frankly to you about feelings. You want to be your child's most trustworthy friend.

Question 33. Tell your child that if anyone, even one of your friends, should try to harm or molest her or him, you want to know about it immediately.

Question 34. Teach your child to watch people when he or she is outside playing. A child should never become so involved in play that he or she fails to notice persons who might make advances toward the child. If the child is playing on the school ground, instruct your child to run to a playground teacher to report any strangers loitering nearby. Explain that if a similar incident occurs at home you want to know about it right away.

Question 35. It is hoped that the child will respond that he or she will report the incident to you immediately. Explain that the person could be looking for an address but that he or she could also be someone who is watching your child with a harmful intent.

Question 36. Answers to the three-part question are as follows:

- Your child should respond that she or he will not accept an invitation to go inside anyone's car or home. Pretend that you are the person extending the invitation. Elicit your child's response, and encourage a firm and certain tone of voice.
- If someone exposes his or her body, tell your child to run. Instruct your child to report the incident to you at once.
- Tell your child never to trade with an adult. Selling scout merchandise is unimportant compared to the child's personal safety.

Question 37. Your dog is a first line of defense against intruders in your home. His sense of smell and hearing are superior to yours. He can often alert you to danger before anything happens.

Question 38. Police advise that you tell your child that he or she should never enter the child's own home if the door has been opened. Teach your child to look for other signs of intrusion such as torn or unlatched screens, misplaced items, or the dog missing from the yard. Instruct your child to go for help to the neighborhood home discussed in Question 27. If the child notices signs of intrusion at home, he or she must go immediately to the safe home you have chosen as a refuge.

Question 39. Teach your child at a young age what drugs can do to destroy a life. Children can be used by molesters to lure other children into dangerous situations. Tell your child never to accept anything that must be put into the body from anyone, even a trusted friend.

Question 40. Instruct your child to tell any offender, even a teacher, that he or she will not have any part of such activities. The answer must be a firm and positive "no!" A teacher should never threaten a student, but if the teacher does make threats, the child should report the incident to you at once. Tell the child that he or she will not flunk the course and that action will be taken against the teacher to protect other students, as well as your child.

Question 41. According to child safety organizations, a molested child should keep telling what has happened until the parents or someone else believes the story and takes action. Reassure your child that you will always listen to his or her complaints of abuse. Assure him or her that you have faith that the child will always tell you the truth about such matters.

Question 42. Encourage your child never to break this important safety rule. You cannot help if you don't know where the child is.

Question 43. Refer to the section on personal identification in Chapter 2.

Question 44. Everyone in our society follows certain rules for safety reasons. You can cite traffic rules to your child as an explanation. Children especially should always obey safety rules because they are more susceptible to harm from others.

Question 45. Refer to Sgt. Frederick Whitley's, and the San Antonio, Texas, Police Department's suggestions on stranger awareness (Chapter 1).

Question 46. Instruct your child to kick, bite, scream for help, and run as fast as possible if accosted. Where the child should turn for help depends on where the child is when the incident occurs. Police advise that if the child is at school, he or she should run to the nearest teacher to report the incident and then go to the school office to report what has happened. If walking home from school in a residential area, the child should run to the nearest house with adults, preferably a house with signs of children, such as toys in the yard. If in a business section, the child should run into an occupied building, report the incident, and use the phone to call the police. Tell your child never to run to a deserted area where a molester can follow. The child must run toward people, screaming for help. Although it would be ideal if the child got away with a complete description of the molester and the license number of the person's car, it is not practical to emphasize identification to the child before safety. Encourage your child to run first and remember later.

Question 47. Police advise these guidelines on telephone awareness. Your child should know to dial "0" for telephone operator in case of needing help. He or she should know the number of the police, fire department, ambulance service, and own area code and phone number. Let your child stop the test now and demonstrate the ability to call for help using these numbers.

Question 48. Explain that it is vital that your child stay with parents or grandparents when in public and *never* leave them for *any* reason.

Question 49. As mentioned earlier, children must be taught *never* to wander, even from home. If a child needs to use the restroom, his or her guardian should accompany the child without complaint. Young boys and girls should never be allowed in a restroom without a guardian. When parents aren't present, a restroom is an ideal place for the sexual molestation of children. To aid a child in knowing what to do in case he or she becomes lost in public, refer to the mall game in Chapter 1.

Question 50. Some child safety organizations feel that children should not be allowed to walk anywhere alone. When supervised, however, children may walk with a group of friends in a place approved by the parents. Continue the discussion, and read the grandmother's story on car safety in Chapter 1.

Chapter 6

The Safety Skills Test

The second part of the written/oral test is an eight- to ten-week skills test in three stages. It should begin in the week following the completion of the written test.

Stage I, *Basic Skills,* is easy to master for both parent and child. Basic skills include communication between the parent and the child's school and between the parent and child. These simple tasks will create an environment of safety awareness within the family. Like the written/oral test, these tasks place the responsibility of safety training upon the parents or guardians of the child.

STAGE I: BASIC SKILLS

Plan to complete the basic skills section in two weeks. Monday you may wish to choose one basic skill from the school section and one from the home section. Thursday you may choose to add another skill from the public section, or you may choose to complete all skills in the public section in one day. Select the skills according to your time and the disposition of the child. You may inform the child that the testing period for skills has begun, but you must not tell when individual tests will occur. Such information could change the child's reaction and the outcome of the tests.

Beside each test there is a space in which to check off results. Mark satisfactory results with a blue or black pen. Mark poor results in red. Red check marks indicate the need to retest at a later date. If there are many children to be tested, mark the child's initial above the check mark to prevent confusion. You may use colored pencils to differentiate a number of children being tested—for example, orange for Anna, blue for Terry, green for Thomas.

After the child has been tested, immediately notify him or her of the type of test given and whether you found the child's reactions satisfactory. Inform the child that there is no failing grade, and invite her or him to discuss the situation. Again, it is vital to review the test and results immediately after test time.

STAGE II: INTERMEDIATE SKILLS

Stage II skills will require more parental effort and planning. Stage II will involve the child, the parents, and the parents' friends. Set-up situations in this stage of training will require friends to place phone calls to the child's home. They must also drive and walk around the child's home area. Use your judgment in selecting friends both known and unknown by your child. They should be well trusted and preferably should have children of their own. Parents may wish to trade acting positions with other parents who plan to test their children, too. Set-up situations will require prearranged times, and parents must always be present, yet preferably out of the child's view. Certain tests may create minor stress in the child, but they should not be allowed to cause extreme fearfulness. If you observe such fear, stop the test and immediately explain the situation to the child. If you handle the test in such a way, it will still be a teaching situation and a positive learning experience.

Set-up situations require that you give your child praise and an explanation immediately following the test. Discuss the test with the acting friend present to help evaluate the child's reaction. All evaluations must be offered in positive terms. For example:

Mother: Mary, I was very proud of you for running to me to report the car that stopped near our house. I'm sure that if it ever happened again you'd tell me even sooner than you did this time. [then addressing the friend] How do you think Mary did on the test?

Friend: I think she did very well. I was pleased to see that she didn't try to speak to me. In a real situation, speaking to a stranger could be very dangerous.

Mother: Mary, how do you feel about the test?

Mary has been well nurtured with praise as well as constructive criticism. She has been told in a positive way to report suspicious incidents sooner than she did on the test. Praise has been offered for what she did do (report the car) and for what she did not do (speak to a stranger). She has also been given time to evaluate her feelings concerning the test.

Plan three to four weeks to complete the tests in Stage II.

STAGE III: ADVANCED SKILLS

Stage III skills are almost all set-up situations. Set up the school test at least one week before the day it is to occur. It is best to make an appointment with the school principal and the child's teacher. Explain the test and its purpose, and plan a test date together. The teacher or principal should be available in the test area so that the child can report the incident. The parent or guardian should be close at hand but out of the child's view completely. After the test is complete, everyone involved should meet to evaluate the results.

Allow three to four weeks to complete the Advanced Skills of Stage III.

The time allotment for the complete safety skills test is eight to ten weeks. It may be completed earlier if possible but should not extend beyond a ten-week period.

The written/oral and skills tests will require planning and effort. Regardless of disappointments, changes in schedule, or sacrifice involved, however, you will be pleased with the outcome. Your child will be aware of dangerous situations and will be trained to aid himself. Your responsibility does not end when the test is over, however. You must continue to be watchful and reinforce good safety habits on a daily basis throughout childhood. Retest your child every two years to reinforce proper safety habits. During the retesting, you may update your test with the latest safety information.

Additional test situations should be added by parents if they fit the needs of the child in a particular home and school environment. The tests given here carry no guarantees. No one can completely ensure the safety of a child. As parents, we can only try our best to equip our children with knowledge and skill, and pray that it will prove useful if the need arises.

STAGE I: BASIC SKILLS
(TWO-WEEK DURATION)

School

Arrange for your child's school to call immediately if child misses class or fails to report to school. ☐

If you cannot pick up your child from school make sure the school receives a signed letter from you *naming* and *describing* the person who will pick him up. ☐

Observe your child. Does he or she arrive home from school on time each day? If not, find out why. ☐

Home

Discuss with your child the need to tell you if she or he doesn't want to be with someone and why. ☐

Discuss with your child the need to tell you if he or she plans to go somewhere and why. ☐

Plan and discuss a distress word with your child that should be used when the child is in trouble or to test individuals who insist you sent them to pick up your child. ☐

Discuss stranger awareness. Include who is a stranger and why he or she is a stranger. Give suggestions to your child about safety around strangers. ☐

Give child a completed ID card or disk. Include name, address, phone number, and emergency numbers. Tape money to the back of the card or disk tag for emergency use only. The child may prefer to carry emergency money taped to the inside of his or her shoes. ☐

Ensure that all curfews are obeyed by your child. ☐

Public

Play the "Stranger" game. Have your child pick out five strangers and tell why they are strangers. Play the game in a busy public area. ☐

Observe your child in public. Does he wander, go to the bathroom or any place alone? Correct this behavior. ☐

STAGE II: INTERMEDIATE SKILLS
(THREE TO FOUR WEEKS' DURATION)

School

Observe your child. Does she or he seem to relate well to other children and want to be with them? If not, correct this behavior by encouraging the child's friends to come to play at your home. Support your child's friendships. Make sure she or he has at least one friend she or he enjoys and stays with on the playground. Is your child gregarious or a loner? If there seems to be a problem, set up an appointment with your child's teacher and encourage his or her help. ☐

Home

Teach your child to use different types of phones correctly. ☐

Instruct your child how you want him or her to use the phone in emergencies. Write emergency numbers on the phone, and practice with your child. ☐

Arrange for your friends to call your home at specified times. Be sure your child is available to answer the phone. Observe how the child answers the callers when they seek different types of information. They should ask questions about the child's and the parents' schedules and whether the parents are at home. ☐

Observe your child answering the door during the coming week. Does he or she refuse to allow anyone entry? Ask your child to pretend to be alone in the house. When someone knocks on the door, does the child refuse to go to the door? ☐

Set up a situation with an adult female or male friend. The friend must drive very slowly around the neighborhood, particularly near the yard where your child will be playing. Does your child notice the slow driver and report it immediately? ☐

Set up a situation with a male adult friend whom your child does not know. Ask the friend to walk around your home at a prearranged time when your child is in the yard. He must carefully watch your child. Does your child notice the man and report him to you immediately? ☐

Teach your child to scream as loud as possible and to use the scream if anyone tries to harm him or take him away. Tell him to bite and kick also. Practice with him during Stage II training. ☐

Public

Does your child correct you if you leave her in the car alone? Does she correct you if you leave her in the car with other children? ☐

STAGE III: ADVANCED SKILLS
(THREE TO FOUR WEEKS' DURATION)

School

Refer to the parents' guide to skills for instructions. Set up a situation with your child's school, with yourself, the principal, a teacher, and a male or female adult friend the child does *not* know. Have the friend offer a ride to your child after school. Your friend must claim that you have been injured in an accident and that you have sent him or her to take the child home. Does the child turn and run immediately? ☐ Does the child converse with the driver? ☐ Does the child get into the car? ☐ Does the child ask for the distress word from the driver? ☐

Observe your child before and after school. Does the child walk too near occupied cars? ☐ Does the child keep a safe distance? ☐

Home

Set up a situation with a male or female neighbor. At a prearranged time, send your child to the neighbor's home on an errand. Have the friend invite your child inside. If the child refuses, have the neighbor insist by saying, for example, "I'll give you some cake. It's okay we will keep it a secret from your mother." Does the child enter the neighbor's home? ☐

Set up a situation with a male friend. At the prearranged time, have the child playing in the yard. The friend should approach your child in a friendly manner and ask the child if he can take a picture of him. Does your child chat with the friend? ☐ Does the child report the friend immediately? ☐ Does the child allow a picture to be taken? ☐ If bribed with candy or toys, does the child allow a picture to be taken? ☐

Arrange a situation with a female friend. At a prearranged time, have the friend drive near your home where your child will be playing in the yard. Have the friend drop toys or a small animal near your home and wait in her car nearby. Does your child leave the yard to investigate? ☐   Does the child speak to the friend if approached? ☐   If bribed, does the child enter the friend's car? ☐

Set up a situation with a male friend. At a prearranged time, when child is in the yard, have the friend drive near, approach your child, and offer a reward of toys or candy if the child will get into his car to help him find his lost rabbit. ☐   Does your child turn and run immediately? ☐   Does the child hesitate and then run? ☐   Does the child chat with the friend? ☐ Does the child accept the bribe then enter the car? ☐

Public

Refer to the mall game in Chapter 1. Take your child to small gift shop, a grocery store, an airport, or a large busy public area. In each setting have your child describe whom he would go to if in trouble. ☐

PART THREE

VITAL INFORMATION

Chapter 7

Your Child's Personal File Folder

Parents should take precautionary measures to ensure that vital information is immediately accessible to authorities in the case of a child who disappears.

Scott Evans, Chief of Police in the Kerrville, Texas, police department, recommends that the following list of information be kept for each child in the family. Evans says, "This information will help to speed a police investigation. It saves a lot of footwork."

- Current full face and profile pictures.
- The child's birth certificate.
- The child's blood type.
- A record of scars or birthmarks.
- A list of any medical problems requiring medication.
- A list of needed medications.
- Unusual speech patterns.
- A description of any physical handicap.
- A list of any allergies.
- Medical record of vaccinations.
- Eye glass prescription and frame type.

- Current directory of school and neighborhood friends.
- Current directories of doctors, teachers, coaches, and so on.
- A description of child's recreational habits.
- A list of places the child frequently goes and their phone numbers.
- Fingerprints.
- Complete set of dental records.
- Bicycle (or other personal vehicle) description and registration number.
- Record of child's written and skills safety test. Weak areas should be marked for retest time. If the child should become an abduction victim, the weak areas in testing could provide a clue as to how the child was taken.
- Child's current distress word.
- The child's complaints and/or identification of individuals who have made questionable advances toward him or her, including any threats, bribes, or incidents of picture taking.
- Search packets. Parents can obtain packets by writing to the National Center for Missing and Exploited Children, 1835 K Street N.W., Suite 700, Washington, DC 20006.

These items may be kept in the child's folder as a precautionary measure to avoid delays in searching if the child should become missing. Keep the folder in a safe place. In the event of an emergency, it can be shared with the authorities to provide them with needed information that can easily be forgotten by parents in stressful times.

Statistically restating the problem of the molested child is overwhelming. It is estimated that one out of every four female children and one out of every ten male children will be molested before adulthood. Yet the number of molested children is difficult to predict because many suspected cases are left unreported.

Statistics alone do not relate the tragedies involved with each abuse. A grandmother recalls her thoughts after her grandchild was raped:

Until it happened to our family I never paid much attention to statistics. Now my grandchild is one of those numbers, and each number represents a little child just like ours.

SLAM (Society's League Against Molestation) is an organization concerned with the many children that these statistics represent. It was founded by Patti Linebaugh in 1980, after the rape and torture murder of her two-year-old granddaughter. The founder reports that the two-year-old child was murdered by a pedophile with a twenty-year record of child molestation. He had been in prison or institutions seven times and was released as a model patient six weeks before the child's death.

SLAM, now in forty-three states, with a membership of 20,000, has proposed the following guidelines to aid parents:

1. No one has the right to touch the private parts of his or her body or to make the child feel uncomfortable. Children have the right to say no.
2. To tell you if anyone asks to or has taken his or her picture.
3. Adults do not come to children for help. Adults ask adults for help.
4. Never go near a car with someone in it. Never get in a car without your permission.
5. To make you aware of any unusual discussions or strange requests.
6. To tell you when any adult asks him or her to keep a "secret."
7. To tell you of being given gifts and/or money.
8. Never to go into someone's home without your knowledge.
9. When away from home, scared, or uncomfortable, your child has the right to use the telephone without anyone's permission.
10. To tell you of any situation in which a statement or gesture is made about sex or love.
11. Never to answer the door when alone.
12. Never admit to anyone over the telephone that they are home alone.

13. You will always believe your child about a molestation and will protect the child from further harm. PARENTS: Please note that children do not lie about molestation.

Parents should also:

- Question money or gifts your child may bring home.
- Ask your child whom he or she is spending time with and what activities they engage in.
- Find out who your child's best friend is and why.
- Be watchful of any strong bond that seems to develop between your child and an adult figure in his or her life (friends, teachers, coaches, clergymen, etc.).
- Avoid male babysitters and any overnight trips alone with an adult.
- Maintain constant and regular telephone contact with your child whenever one of you is away from home.
- Never leave your child unattended, day or night.
- Never leave your child alone in a car—even if it's only for a few minutes.
- Be involved in any sports or activities your child engages in.
- Beware of coaches or leaders who do not have a child of their own in the same group.
- Listen when your child tells you that he or she does not want to be or go with someone. There may be a reason why.
- Never make your child submit to physical contact (i.e., hugs and kisses, etc.) if the child does not want to. A child has the right to say no.
- No one should want to be with your child more than you. When someone is showing your child too much attention, ask yourself why.
- Be sensitive to any changes in your child's behavior or attitudes. Encourage an open communication with your child. Never belittle any fear or concern your child may express to you. Never compromise any private or confidential matter your child may share with you.

If your child has been molested:

Take your child to a private place and ask what happened.

This is a gesture of love. Speak to your child and allow him or her to share feelings with you. It is embarrassing to a molested child to be confronted in public. The warmth of a familiar atmosphere and the presence of an understanding parent are vital for relaxation at this time. Feelings will surface more easily in this environment. However, the ideal is not always possible. Allow children to share vital information as they offer it, regardless of the privacy available.

Tell your child you are sorry this happened and that you will protect him or her from further molestation.

Parental statements of sympathy and protection should be offered to a molested child. Because child molesters often use threats, children should be assured that no future harm will come to them. Discuss any threats or bribes that were used by the molester and explain to your child what you intend to do to protect him or her. Explain to your child that threats are words. Words cannot do harm without actions. Let your child know that you will not allow anyone to take action to harm him or her.

Respect your child's privacy. Discuss the incident with trusted friends only and never in front of the child.

Friends and relatives may crowd your home to get the facts about what happened, but don't encourage them. Assure them that everything is being handled properly, and ask them to leave. If you must discuss the molestation with someone, choose a relative, close friend, or clergyman who will not repeat the story. Never discuss the incident in your child's presence. Your child deserves to have his or her dignity protected.

Notify authorities, even if

The decision to notify authorities will be

SLAM guideline	*Explanation*
the molester is a friend or relative. By doing this you may save another child from being victimized.	especially difficult if the molester is close to your family. But remember that most molesters don't stop after abusing only one child. Your failure to notify the police will give the molester the support he or she needs to continue harming children.
Be supportive of your child. Demonstrate that your love, regard, and respect for him or her has not been diminished or altered by the experience whether or not he or she had been tricked, lured, or forced to participate.	Your child must know that you still cherish him or her. Your support must consist of providing time to talk, spiritual guidance, medical care, good nutrition, your presence at home, and possibly professional counseling. Isolation from well-meaning but intrusive friends should be provided.
Make sure your child understands fully that the blame and responsibility rest with the molester. Many children carry a great burden of fear and guilt after an attack. Children worry that it was somehow their fault, especially if they continued contact with the molester after the first incident.	Be sure that your child knows that he or she is completely innocent of any wrongdoing. Children should not be made to feel guilty because of a molestation. The sexual offender is completely to blame, especially if the person made further contact with the child. Reaffirm that you love and believe in your child and that he or she should not feel fearful or guilty because of what has happened.
Emphasize that your child did the right thing in telling you about the incident. Be aware that most molesters frighten children into silence by threats. They tell children that their parents will not love them any more if the parent should ever learn of what the child has done.	Explain to your child that you will love her or him forever. Nothing that has happened will change your deep feelings for the child, regardless of what anyone else says.

SLAM guideline	*Explanation*
Offer support, comfort, and sympathy without overreacting to the point that the child is frightened more by your reaction than by the incident itself.	Parents should show their concern but never in extreme. Violent outbursts or threats of physical revenge will terrify an already frightened child. Remain as calm as possible, and allow your child to continue expressing his or her feelings.
Be sure your child realizes that you believe what he or she has told you.	Perhaps no point is more important than this one. It is vital that you believe and accept the molested child's story. Authorities in the field of child abuse emphasize that children rarely lie about being sexually abused. Your belief in your child will strengthen his or her trust in you
Be aware that your child has been lured, tricked, or forced into doing something that causes deep confusion and a strong sense of guilt and shame.	A child does not walk away in a carefree manner from being sexually abused. The incident will haunt him or her daily until it is resolved. Mentally note that such abuses are planned by molesters to cause children to harbor feelings of anger and remorse.
Maintain an open communication with your child regarding the incident. Do not pressure a child into talking.	When channels of communication are open between a parent and child, deep feelings will have a way to be shared. This expression is a healthy one and should not be forced. Prying information from a child will further reduce his or her feeling of dignity and self-worth.
Please do not make these types of statements: "I told you to come straight home." "Why did you keep going back?" "Mr. Jones is such a respected man; you must be making this up." These statements will cause your child to feel more blame and more shame about the incident.	An acceptable approach in speaking with a molested child is to make an observation, express your feelings, state your intentions, and encourage a response.

SLAM guideline

Determine if your child has been physically injured and is in need of medical attention. Do not hesitate to seek professional counseling, for the entire family if necessary, after a child has undergone a sexual attack.

When choosing a counselor, take into consideration that many have little knowledge in this area. Inquire as to the number of molestation victims they have worked with, type of treatment, and any other questions or doubts you might have. If your child is showing behavioral problems, unusual fears, or you feel he or she needs counseling, and a counselor says he or she is too young—find another counselor. If your child has been molested over a period of time and a counselor tells you he or she is all right after one or two counseling sessions—find another counselor.

You can be reimbursed for the cost of counseling through the Victim Aid Program in your District Attorney's office.

Explanation

Authorities suggest that it is best to take the child to a hospital's emergency room or a private physician after a molestation. Do not remove any clothing or bathe the child. Legal evidence can be destroyed by such measures. Have the doctor look for signs of sexual abuse, and request that evidence be saved or recorded for legal purposes.

Several types of counselors are available. Parents may investigate professionals in the field of child abuse or turn to rape crisis centers for aid. Your state's Department of Human Resources may be able to videotape your child's giving his or her account of the molestation and offer it as court evidence. Perhaps the most overlooked and effective counseling tool comes from the clergy. Roger Bonnett, a bishop of the Church of Jesus Christ of Latter-Day Saints, comments on counseling techniques: "All the training that you and I can take from a classroom is not enough. Knowledge itself doesn't do it. You need the knowledge but coupled with common sense and love. I go back to the old quotation that people don't care how much you know until they know how much you care."

Extra information about reimbursements can be obtained through rape crisis units, your police department, or community mental health centers.

Chapter 8

What Every Parent Should Know

Chris Avery, M.D., director of the Humana Hospital Emergency Room in San Antonio, Texas, explains:

In most cases of sexual abuse there may be nothing obvious about the presentation. It's more the subtleness of the complaints. There is a kind of hopelessness and fear, and I can sense the child is coming to me for help.

Children feel that if they can get an excuse to come see a physician or some other professional the professional will somehow uncover the problem of sexual abuse. It's very hard for children to come forward and tell what has happened to them. Too often, prolonged sexual abuse occurs because parents aren't willing to believe the child is telling the truth. Children usually don't feign illness with this type of complaint. When they tell you something, as shocking as it may be, you'd better listen to them immediately.

Outlining the sexual signs of abuse by age groups has bearing. Baby-toddler signs are frequently more obvious due to the size of the child. In the school-age child one of the signs that is most prominent is a change in performance. Any emotional change from the ordinary is the tipoff. New and unusual generalized fears, such as fear of the dark, or being left alone, are common. The dominant teenage sign is depression. But again, depression can be a sign of almost anything because the teenage years are difficult years of adjustment. Lack of interest in dating is another big sign in this age group.

Signs of sexual abuse can be signs of other problems too, but parents should be familiar with this list.

Doctor Avery and Yolanda Rodriguez-Escobar, a specialist in child protective services with the Texas Department of Human Resources, recommend that parents be aware of the following signs of sexual abuse:

From birth through three years of age, a child may

- show signs of physical injury.
- show signs of physical illness, possibly related to genital or urinary systems.
- become unusually fussy.
- refuse his or her favorite food.
- become extremely shy.
- exhibit a sudden or unusual fear of strangers.
- show a lack of enjoyment of his or her favorite playthings.
- cling to parents as if fearful.
- experience great difficulty getting to sleep.
- exhibit extreme fear of being left alone.
- suffer from frightening dreams.
- regress to an earlier pattern of behavior.
- show a regression of skills.
- experience a loss of his or her sense of security.
- become unable to adjust to his or her normal schedule.
- manifest any change from his normal behavior pattern.

From age four through twelve, a child may

- exhibit signs of physical injury.
- manifest signs of physical illness, with a variety of symptoms from recurrent headaches, upset stomach or urinary tract infection.
- exhibit sudden extreme shyness.

- suffer from frightening dreams.
- experience great difficulty getting to sleep.
- refuse his or her favorite foods.
- suffer from depression.
- exhibit some loss of memory.
- worry excessively, interrupting his or her normal life pattern.
- exhibit a change in his or her level of scholastic achievement.
- exhibit fear of specific adults.
- have a sudden and unwarranted fear of the dark.
- exhibit extreme fear of being alone.
- show a regression in patterns of behavior or skills.
- exhibit a change in school relationships, including possible fighting and the sudden inability to adjust.
- show a lack of enjoyment of his or her favorite TV shows, movies, games, or other activities.
- seem easily distracted as though his or her mind is wandering.
- manifest a change in his or her normal attitude.
- manifest a change in his or her pattern of normal behavior.
- act out in a sexual manner appearing more knowledgeable about sex than his or her peers.
- develop a pseudomature character, taking over specific parental responsibilities in the home (a sign predominantly associated with incest).

*From age thirteen through nineteen,
a teenager may*

- manifest signs of physical injury.
- manifest signs of physical illness, headache, stomach cramps, urinary tract infections.
- suddenly refuse food.
- suffer from sudden and violent frightening dreams.
- manifest difficulty in getting to sleep.
- seem in the depths of depression.
- exhibit an inability to concentrate.

- show irritability or manifest angry outbursts toward others.
- exhibit a sudden and unwarranted fear of the dark.
- have a sudden lapse of enjoyment of dating.
- feel an unexplainable fear of being left alone.
- worry excessively, interrupting his or her normal life patterns.
- experience a loss of memory.
- exhibit fear of specific adults.
- exhibit a change in his or her level of scholastic achievement.
- act out the sexual encounter with siblings or friends.
- experience a lack of enjoyment for his or her favorite activities.
- make an attempt to run away from home.
- contemplate suicide.
- appear passive or overly compliant in behavior.
- behave seductively with the opposite sex.
- manifest a deviation from his or her normal behavior patterns or attitudes.

PART FOUR

MISSING:
WHAT TO DO?

Chapter 9

Missing Children

The epidemic international problem of missing children is proportionate to our lack of knowledge in the area. Even today, the subject of vanished persons—both adults and children—is barely emerging from the shadows of the unknown into the dim light of understanding. They are the nameless faces, the faceless names, and the statistics that astound the public.

In the United States alone, available figures vary drastically as to the number of missing children a year. Perhaps this variance is caused by the low percentage of police departments that list missing persons with the NCIC (National Crime Information Center). According to an FBI spokesman at the NCIC headquarters in Washington, DC, their relationship with the nation's police departments is strictly cooperative.

Many parents become distraught when the police refuse to begin a search for their child because of a twenty-four- to forty-eight-hour waiting period. It is difficult for the parents to understand why local authorities do not make an immediate listing with the NCIC. The refusal is in part a result of the tremendous number of runaways each year, many of whom return of their own accord within forty-eight hours after disappearing. If a parent wishes, however, he or she can bypass the police department and contact a local FBI office to request an immediate listing. According to the NCIC, this national missing person file is primarily for identification purposes in the case of a deceased victim. However, it can also be used to identify living victims who are unable to do so themselves.

The Federal Bureau of Investigation in Washington, DC, furnished this list of NCIC computer categories and statistics.

- *Catastrophe*—lists missing victims of any age. Fires and floods are examples of the catastrophic category.

- *Disability*—lists missing persons any age who are suffering from a proven physical or mental disability, including senility, who subject themselves or others to an immediate danger. An elderly person or a mentally retarded child who wanders away are examples of the disability category.

- *Endangered*—lists missing persons of any age in the company of another person under circumstances indicating personal danger. A father and son who disappear on a camping trip and don't return home when expected is an example of the endangered category.

- *Involuntary*—lists missing persons of any age who disappear under circumstances that indicate their leaving was not voluntary. Kidnapping is an example of the involuntary category.

- *Juvenile*—lists missing persons who are not declared emancipated by the laws of their resident state and who do not meet the criteria for inclusion in the other four categories.

The total for the five categories in 1983 was 189,532. The 1983 end-of-the-year balance resulted in 182,374 entries being removed as a result of locating the victim or cancelling the entry. When a child reaches the age of emancipation according to the laws of his or her resident state, the entry is automatically cancelled. However, the young victim may be listed again in another category if the police department or FBI choose to make an entry.

In contrast, the National Center for Missing and Exploited Children brochure indicates that as many as a million or more persons, mostly children, enter the ranks of the missing each year. These phenomenal and differing figures show a definite lack of communication between organizations and a significant need for a systematic method of accurately calculating the total numbers of missing persons, especially children. This could come in the form of a state-by-state effort to require an accounting of statistics before they are entered by that state into the NCIC categories.

In addition to the problem of conflicting statistics, there is not a specialized category at the NCIC for missing children. They are listed in any of the five categories whose entry requirements they fit. A possible solution to this problem would be the establishment of a specialized children's category. Divisions such as parental kidnapping, stranger abduction, runaways, and sexual exploitation involving pornography and prostitution could be included. Another advance suggested by child safety organizations would be the requirement that all police departments submit entries on all missing children, foregoing the twenty-four- to forty-eight-hour waiting period. This would ensure that each child would be listed for identification purposes, regardless of how the child disappeared.

By the end of each year, accurate statistics would be available to specify nationwide the number of children listed in each division. Such vital information would enable the government to present facts proving the need for the following:

- Trained task forces specializing in the investigation of and search for missing children.
- Laws to protect children adequately and to discourage criminals before they act.
- Funds to help support organizations that are pioneers in the field of missing children.

The National Center for Missing and Exploited Children brochure estimates that of the million children reported missing each year it is supposed that most of these are runaways. The current attitude toward runaways is one of lassitude. Many times they do not rate an investigation into their disappearance regardless of the potential street threat of sexual exploitation.

Statistics from the National Center indicate that noncustodial parental abductions account for at least 25,000 disappearances, yet the numbers may be as high as 500,000. Many of these children are exposed to abusive situations, and some are murdered by the offending parent.

According to the National Center for Missing and Exploited Children brochure, at least 20,000 disappearances remain unsolved by the end of each year. Incredible numbers of families are left battered by the ordeal of children missing from their homes. These figures cannot account for the devastation of millions of youngsters who are robbed of the chance to reach a healthy and productive adulthood.

Often implicated in these disappearances is a criminal element responsible for the deliverance of children into pornography and prostitution. These highly organized rings net multimillion dollar rewards for the criminals involved. Yet the monetary factor is only a by-product of the perverse sexual satisfaction received by offenders who use children to gratify their own fantasies. Pedophiles profess that in the United States there are millions of men who are sexually drawn to boys. The probability of attraction to female children by pedophiles is likely to be as great.

The pedophile communication network covers a vast territory with possible international boundaries. It may serve millions on this wide scope, as a result of the pedophile's basic ability to dominate and manipulate.

The pedophile's success is due in part to the availability of abandoned, neglected, and runaway children who are often treated as forgotten castoffs. The pedophile segment of society is keenly aware that law enforcement is unable to keep track of these countless lost souls and that few steps may be taken to investigate their disappearances. Encouraged by this knowledge, a low-key pedophile operator is able to completely infiltrate any aspect of a child's life. He may turn out to be the Boy Scout leader who starts a prostitution ring, threatening the victims into silence. The pedophile could also be an outstanding citizen using his or her job involving children to exploit them in pornography. Once entrapped, the child can become entangled in an organized web of sexual acts that can lead to disappearance or death. This type of individual should not be considered sick. Quite the contrary, he or she has a skillful and well-organized manner of operation. In addition to producing child porn magazines, the underground world of pedophiles has its own literature to aid followers in obtaining victims and pleading legal cases if they are caught. Such thorough and intricate organization, capable of spreading child sexual exploitation to a global level, does not come from a sick mind but rather a criminal one.

Perhaps because of the desire to see justice served, Americans have become confused as to who is the real victim of this abuse. Defenses often used by offenders include gaining sympathy by feigning mental illness or pleading that they are outstanding citizens who could not have engaged in any such activity. One woman victimized as a child claims, "No one would believe what I had to say about him. He must be intelligent because he has worked himself into the community very well. He is above reproach in everyone's eyes, except those of his victims."

The delicate balance of child rights can easily be destroyed by advocates for sexual liberation of the young. The children's defense lies in the hands of parents, who must be certain that their beliefs and attitudes are reflected by the law.

Chapter 10

What to Do if Your Child Disappears

When parents face the horror of having a child suddenly disappear, there are certain steps they can take that will aid in investigation. Betty DiNova, executive director of the Dee Scofield Awareness Program, has provided that agency's guidelines for parents to follow in the case of a missing child.

THE DEE SCOFIELD CHECKLIST

When a child under age eighteen disappears, it is important to take action immediately, even if you suspect the child may have left voluntarily. Runaways who are not streetwise, and even so-called incorrigibles who can fend for themselves quite well, often become victims of street criminals. Therefore, parents should insist on a thorough official investigation. Minor children are not held legally accountable for their decisions and therefore should not be left in a position in which they must make crucial decisions on which their very lives may depend. The following fifteen steps will help you to take appropriate action.

1. *File a missing persons report.* File a report with your local police or sheriff, as appropriate. Also file a report with the Salvation Ar-

my's Department of Missing Persons, 120 W. 14th Street, New York, NY 10011, as soon as you have checked all personal sources of information as to where the child might be. Be truthful in reporting family conflicts and/or relationships or other unpleasant circumstances. Authorities are crucially handicapped if they do not have all the facts and circumstances leading up to the disappearance. Ask yourself which is more important . . . your pride or your child's life.

2. *Ask the authorities in your jurisdiction to register data* with the National Crime Information Center (NCIC) and your State Bureau of Investigation. Follow up with a call to your nearest FBI office to verify entry in the NCIC computer in Washington, DC. They will enter it for you if the police have failed to do so.

3. *Stay in close touch with the jurisdictional authorities.* Insist that they follow up on all leads to your satisfaction. Don't bother them unnecessarily (which would hinder the search), but do check with them periodically *on an unscheduled basis.*

4. *Insist that authorities accept all outside offers of help.* Leave no stone unturned. Don't *assume* that they are giving highest priority to the search for your child. Ongoing crimes take precedence, and most police are apathetic about missing children because they assume them all to be runaways.

5. *Offer a reward and distribute posters.* On the posters put the child's photo and description, the contact telephone number, and/or the address. Ask your police department to help you with this. Include the child's age, the date and place the child was last seen, and the basic circumstances of the disappearance.

6. *If your child does not return within twenty-four hours* and there is no indication that the child ran away, ask your jurisdictional police agency to request an FBI investigation. The Federal Kidnapping Statute provides that when a victim is not released within twenty-four hours, it can be presumed he or she has been taken across a state line. If the police refuse to request it, or if the FBI refused to comply with the request, call or write the Dee Scofield Awareness Program, giving all details—especially any that might indicate an abduction has occurred or that the child has been taken across the state line. The Dee Program will seek an FBI investigation on your behalf. (This pertains to parental kidnaps as well. The FBI is

authorized by the Parental Kidnapping Prevention Act of 1980 to search for abducted children taken across state lines.)

7. *Keep a pencil and paper by the telephone* to record any information received. If possible, have a tape recorder handy to record messages and voices.

8. *Publicize the missing child's photo and disappearance date everywhere possible.* Include as many national directories of missing persons you can. If the child is alive or in circulation, someone might recognize the resemblance and contact the authorities. Or the child might see the story and call home. If the child did run away, your concern could have a positive effect on him or her.

9. *Call runaway hotlines.* See if your child has left a message for you, or you can leave a message for your child. Indicate a willingness to listen to your child's viewpoint.

10. *Check morgues and hospitals* in your area for unidentified children or bodies.

11. *Contact the Bergen County Missing Persons Bureau,* Hackensack, NJ, and the Colorado Bureau of Investigation in Denver to register the details and photo of the missing child. Both these agencies maintain computerized information on unidentified bodies.

12. *Report all uncooperative and/or negligent law enforcement personnel* and other officials to the Dee Scofield Awareness Program, which will report your complaints to appropriate authorities if warranted and warn other searching parents in their areas.

13. *If you use a private detective,* be careful to obtain a reputable one. The Scofield program does not make any recommendations but will upon request furnish names and addresses of any known private investigators in your area. However, the program personnel urge you to check with the Better Business Division of your Chamber of Commerce before making a financial commitment to any private detective agency.

14. *If your child is a suspected runaway, or is over eighteen,* some of the following steps might also be appropriate, depending on the age of the child and the circumstances:
    - Check Social Security records. This may have to be done by your congressman.
    - Check with State Department, the Passport Division, 1425 K Street, NW, Washington, DC 20524.

- Check with your state's motor vehicle registration department (if a car is involved). If your city or county is a member of the computer service, this can be done almost instantaneously. If not, you must write to the motor vehicle bureau in your state capital.
- If your child is a college graduate, contact the college's job placement office to see if anyone has called or written the college for a transcript or reference. Also contact the alumni association of the college for any address changes for your child.
- If your child is old enough to join the armed services, check with local recruiting offices and the national headquarters of each service.
- If a missing adult is in a profession that requires a license by state or union, check with the appropriate agency in each state. Ask your library for addresses.
- Check past telephone bills of missing adults for out-of-town numbers that might indicate a destination of the missing person.
- Check credit cards for out-of-town purchases that may have been made by the missing person or an abductor.

15. *If your child is a victim of parental kidnapping,* many of the foregoing steps may not apply. Write The Dee Scofield Awareness Program for the legal steps you can take, based on your state laws.

INDEPENDENT HELP AGENCIES FOR FAMILIES OF MISSING CHILDREN

Most family-formed action agencies began because of the loss of a child as a result of murder or abduction. These organizations began as early as 1975 and had a tendency to specialize in different aspects of the problem of missing children. Some of the first agencies formed were the following:

- Families and Friends of Missing Persons
- The Society for Young Victims

- The Dee Scofield Awareness Program
- Parents of Murdered Children
- Stolen Children Information Exchange
- Child Find
- Find-Me

Dozens of new agencies have emerged, taking their place among the groups to which parents may turn in an emergency. Each action organization has in common the ongoing need for public support. The withdrawal of funds would close many groups that have successfully contributed aid to hundreds of thousands of families and children.

It is inevitable that although some organizations will continue to exist after many years, others will stop their work in the field. Keep this in mind as you survey the following list of available agencies, which was provided by John and Louise Clinkscales of Find-Me, Inc.

- Abducted Children Information Center, Harvey Morse, 1470 Gene Street, Winter Park, FL 32789; 305–831–2000. A computerized registry for missing and abducted children operated at no charge by Locater's International, Inc.
- Adam Walsh Child Resource Center, Inc., Sharon McMorris, 1876 N. University Dr., Ft. Lauderdale, FL 33322; 305–475–4847. Working for missing, abused, and neglected children.
- Bay Area Center for Victims of Child Stealing, Georgia K. Hilegman, Director, 1165 Meridian Ave., Ste. 112, San Jose, CA 95125. Chapters: South Bay 408–247–0195 or South Bay 408–248–3366; North Bay 707–544–6536; East Bay 415–829–9126; Diablo Valley 415–945–1601. This is a nonprofit organization that has been in existence for four years. They provide support, suggestions, referrals, hotlines, monthly meetings, and letter-writing campaigns for any parents of a missing child. The organization provides training and education to law enforcement agencies and the public. It also develops and distributes brochures about missing children and tries to have pictures of missing children aired on TV. They ask for a $20.00 annual membership fee but will not turn away anyone in need.

- Bergen County Missing Persons Bureau, 1 Court St., Hackensack, NJ 07601; 201–646–5750. Maintains perhaps the largest data bank in the United States on unidentified bodies.
- Bureau of Lost Friends & Relations, The, Dr. John Maples, 2730 Arden Way, Suite 138, Sacramento, CA 95825; 916–971–9782.
- Bureau of Missing Children, Inc., John L. Russell, III, P.O. Box 2461, Tampa, FL 33601; 813–879–8580. A nonprofit charity engaged in the location of missing children and the prevention of crimes against children. It currently receives 7847 hours of donated investigative services valued at $283,000 from 122 private investigative agencies serving nineteen states and four countries. It also receives fourteen hours of donated legal services valued at $1450. The advisory board consists of fifty-nine top legislators and law enforcement officers. The organization accepts criminal cases of stranger abductions and parental kidnapping. Cases of runaways are not accepted, but this organization will refer parents to other organizations.
- California Department of Justice, The, State of California, Department of Justice, Special Services Program, 4949 Broadway, Sacramento, CA 95820; 916–739–5114. Has set up a Dental Identification Unit in an effort to identify the more than 300 unidentified bodies on file. Send information on your case to Paul Pane or Steven Wong.
- Child Find, Inc., Gloria Yerkovich, Executive Director, P.O. Box 277, New Paltz, NY 12561; 914–255–1848. Distributes the Child Find directory of missing children to school officials. (The cost of the directory is $10, but if institutions cannot afford the fee, a complimentary copy will be sent.) There is no restriction on photocopying the directory. Child Find encourages the reproduction and far-reaching distribution of its directory of missing children. They maintain a toll-free hot line, 1–800–431–5005, for the identification of a missing child, and they keep a computerized cross-reference of missing children. Their business line is 1–914–255–1848 for parents who need counseling or referrals, or who wish to register a missing child. They sponsor Missing Children's Day every year on May 25 and cooperate with all other existing, viable organizations.
- Center for the Family in Transition, Dorothy Huntington, 5725

Paradise Dr., Bldg. A, Suite 100, Corte Medera, CA 94925; 415–924–5750.

- Child Find of Utah, Inc., Dorothy Williams, 1009 East 4555 South, Salt Lake City, UT 84117; 801–262–8056; Maurine Walker, 5755 Hansen Cir., Murray, UT 84107; 801–261–4134. This organization counsels families and distributes pictures of missing children. They work to inform children and adults of the toll-free Child Find hot line in New York (1–800–431–5005). They hold a yearly fund-raising benefit for Child Find on May 25, Missing Children's Day. They have public information booths at malls, fairs, and the like, and they fingerprint children. Branches are the following: Friends of Child Find of Maine and Massachusetts, John Lawrence Cyr, Jr., 189 Oxford St., Suite 4, Lynn, MA 01901; 617–595–4277. Friends of Child Find of Montana, Joyce J. Kenney, 725 S. Billings Blvd. No. 0, Billings, MT 59101; 406–259–6999. Friends of Missing Children, Kenneth Lawson, Box 8848, Madison, WI 53708; 608–635–4753. Friends of Child Find of Oregon, Inc., Anne Lantry–Brown, President, P.O. Box 756, Springfield, OR 97477–0131; 503–341–3822. Information and referral service for searching families that creates public awareness of child abduction through presentations and prevention materials. Available on a 24-hour basis.

- Child Industries, Michael Meredith, P.O. Box 26814, Salt Lake City, UT 84126; 801–298–2902.

- Child Search, Robert Cohen, 6 Beacon St., Suite 600, Boston, MA 02108; 617–720–1760.

- Children's Rights of Florida, Inc., Kathy Rosenthal, P.O. Box 173, Pinellas Park, FL 33566; 813–546–1593. A nonprofit organization dedicated to helping parents to locate and/or recover their abducted children, both abductions by parents and by strangers. They also aid in finding runaways. Their goal is to bring all missing children home to safety. They work within the legal system to aid parents in dealing with the red tape that is so often encountered in dealing with this problem. They support proposed legislation and constantly update awareness of new legislation passed to aid the searching parent.

- Children's Rights of New York, Inc., John Gill, 19 Maple Ave., Stony Brook, NY 11790; 516–751–7840. Conducts public education and awareness programs on prevention of cruelty to children. Advocates rights of children in legal proceedings. Counsels parents whose children have been abducted by an ex-spouse. Provides advice and referral services to other agencies involved with locating missing or abducted children. Publishes "Hotline," a newsletter with information on legislation concerning missing children and on support groups and their activities.

- Children's Rights of Pennsylvania, Inc., Tom Watts and Charles Blickhahn, Co-Directors, P.O. Box 2764, Lehigh Valley, PA 18001; 215–437–2971. This organization's goal is to aid parents and guardians in finding their missing children. It puts together and circulates an up-to-date picture exhibit of children who have been abducted either by a parent or an unknown person. Photographs and information should be sent to the above address.

- Cobra Connection, Don Bennafield, P.O. Box 1958, Station A, Canton, OH 44705–0958; 216–454–9109. Publishes and distributes forty-six-page manual, "Save a Child," that informs, instructs, creates awareness of the missing-child phenomenon, and teaches prevention. Makes public appearances showing photographs of missing children on television and other media outlets.

- Dee Scofield Awareness Program, Inc., Betty DiNova, 4418 Bay Court Ave., Tampa, FL 33611; 813–839–5025. Provides free search guidance and photo publicity to families of vanished children (nonparental kidnaps), free educational and prevention literature, photo exhibits, and fingerprinting. Serves as a watchdog of public officials. Pays no salaries or rent, subsisting solely on donations that are used exclusively for services. Is a sponsor of Family Reunion Month.

- E.C.H.O., Linda Broadus, P.O. Box 18145, Louisville, KY 40218; 502–637–8761. E.C.H.O. (Exploited Children's Help Organization) is a nonprofit organization of concerned parents and professionals determined to increase public awareness and initiate action in dealing with criminally abused children. They plan to promote legislation in protection of children on both a state and federal level, to provide information and preventive education to the community about the needs and the problems of these children, and offer support to parents of abused or missing children.

- Families and Friends of Missing Persons and Violent Crime Victims, Linda L. Barker, Executive Director, 11051 34th Ave., N.E.,

Seattle, WA 98125; 206–362–1081. Aids families of missing persons during time of search. Offers peer counseling for victims of abduction and their families. Offers twenty-four-hour crisis line. Has chapters in Nevada, Washington, and Ohio.

- Find-Me, Inc., John and Louise Clinkscales, P.O. Box 1612, LaGrange, GA 30241–1612; 404–884–7419. An information center for families with a missing member. Counsels families and promotes awareness and information to media and public. Interested in disappearances of persons of all ages and types. Specializes in older teens and adults—a group that is given the least attention and concern by the media and the public. Publishes *Action* booklet. Sponsors Family Reunion Month. Has no payroll or other administrative expense, therefore 100 percent of their receipts is used in promoting awareness of and solutions to the missing persons phenomenon. Makes annual report to contributors. The Clinkscales are out of their office a considerable amount of time, making contacts and promoting this awareness. If you do not get an answer the first time you try to reach them, keep calling, or write to them.

- F.O.L.K. (Find Our Lost Kids, Inc.), Laurie L. Bambini, 11 Myrtle St., Everett, MA 02149. New and expanding support group serving Eastern Massachusetts.

- Gallery 345/Art for Social Change, Inc., Karin Di Ghia, 345 Lafayette St., New York, NY 10012; 212–535–4797. This organization's project, "Children in Crisis," promotes awareness through exhibits of missing children, teens, and young adults. You may submit information and photographs of your children free of charge. The exhibit can be used by any group as an awareness project. There is no charge other than that for shipping. Does not include parental child-snatching.

- H.E.A.R.T., Leslie Campbell, P.O. Box 1372, Kalamazoo, MI 49005. A Michigan-based, self-help and referral service for families victimized by parental child-snatchings. Concentration on awareness and prevention programs, legislative lobbying, lay counseling, and gathering statistics. Cooperates with similar organizations nationwide that are working for the common cause.

- Hide and Seek Foundation, Inc., Linda and Ernie Rivers, 503–472–4333; Virginia Moyer, 503–472–3717; P.O. Box 806, McMinnville, OR 97128. Hide and Seek Help Line: 503–472–

4333. Branches are the following: Hide and Seek of Fairbanks, Robert and Julie Parzick, Sr., Box 80292, Fairbanks, AK 99701; 907–488–3591; Hide and Seek of Camden County, Jim and Nikki Thoman, 150 Berlin Rd., Gibbsboro, NJ 08026; 609–783–3101; Hide and Seek of Pennsylvania, Mike and Barbette Burd, % Woodward Caves, Woodward, PA 16882; 814–349–5185. The Hide and Seek organization provides crisis counseling and assists victimized families. It is a nonprofit organization that undertakes an investigation of each individual case at no cost to the searching family. It offers crisis counseling and promotes awareness through public speaking to schools, organizations, churches, and clubs. It supports legislation for children's rights and budget increases for law enforcement agencies to add the additional manpower needed to help locate missing children. It supports legislation against child stealing and accepts donations, gifts, and grants.

- Jan Russell, P.O. Box 7341, Chicago, IL 60680–7341. Presentations on the Prevention of Parental Kidnappings. Workshops for searching parents. A booklet, "Parental Kidnapping: A Guide for the Left-Behind Parent," can be ordered by sending $3.50 plus $1.00 for first class postage to the address given.

- Kyle's Story, Louise and John Clinkscales, 205 North Chilton Ave., LaGrange, GA 30240; 404–884–7419. Supplements Find-Me in areas in which Find-Me is prohibited by IRS regulations from working. Assists in publishing *Action* booklet. The organization is named for "Kyle's Story: Friday Never Came: The Search for Missing People," which relates the problems that were encountered in getting officials and the general public to accept the possibility that the disappearance of a college student could forestall a problem. NBC called "Kyle's Story" "one of the best overall treatments of 'the missing phenomenon.' " The only difference between Find-Me and Kyle's Story is that Find-Me's activity is controlled by IRS regulations on tax-exempt activity; Kyle's Story is not.

- Minnesota Missing Kids Action Agency, Patricia Crosby, Director, 320–A, 310 E. 38th St., Minneapolis, MN 55407. A nonprofit, tax-exempt agency with three main goals: public education, physical safety program, and visitation monitoring. The main focus is prevention, followed by assisting searching parents with information and assistance. M.M.K.A.A. currently is sponsoring a bill to make child snatching a form of child abuse and supporting the upgrading of Minnesota abduction laws. Meetings are held monthly. Support groups meet every two weeks.

- Missing Children . . . Help Center, Ivana DiNova, 410 Ware Blvd., Suite 1101, Tampa, FL 33619; 813–681–HELP and 813–623–KIDS. This is a nationwide coordinating agency for families of missing children through reference and referral. It has a speakers' bureau to educate the public, and it has two twenty-four-hour emergency telephone lines. It distributes vital posters of missing children nationwide. All its services are free.

- Missing Children Nationwide, Inc., Alfie Brisben, P.O. Box 5331, Hudson, FL 33568; 813–856–5144.

- Missing Children of America, Inc., Nancy Barros, P.O. Box 10–1938, Anchorage, AK 99510; 907–243–8484. A national network to locate missing children. Educates through seminars and workshops. Locates through referrals to detectives. Helps to identify missing children through use of the "Know Your Child" package.

- Missing Teens and Young Adults, Eileen Luboff, P.O. Box 7800, Santa Cruz, CA 95061; 408–425–3663 and 408–426–7972.

- Nation Wide Missing Persons Bureau, Mildren Stoerner, 3500 Aldine Bender, Box A, Houston, TX 77032; 713–449–0355 and 713–449–3449.

- National Association for Missing Children, Inc., Ellie Hochhauser, Executive Coordinator, 449 North University Dr., Plantation, FL 33324; 305–473–6126. Organization instructs parents about the preventive measures necessary to safeguard children against abduction. Provides step-by-step search and recovery method if a child should become missing. The National Association for Missing Children offers a five-part "Child-Safe" program. For information call 305–473–6126 (Florida residents) or 800–334–0090 (out-of-state residents).

- National Child Search, Inc., Pearla Kinsey-Peterson, P.O. Box 800038, Oklahoma City, OK 73180; 405–685–5621. A national organization that aids in the search and location of children who are missing through parental or stranger abduction or running away. Provides the child's parents with emotional support and guidance. Works with all law enforcement agencies across the

United States and also with any organization concerned with missing children. Promotes legislation regarding missing children. Promotes awareness. Has established a good relationship with law enforcement agencies and media throughout the United States. Donations are appreciated, but there is no charge for services.

- National Missing Children's Locate Center, Inc., John R. Benneth, P.O. Box 42584, Portland, OR 97242; 503–238–1350. Publishes *The Children's Action Network Directory* and sponsors Family Reunion Month.

- Oklahoma's Abducted Children, Inc., Dean O'Donnell, P.O. Box 21326, Oklahoma City, OK 73120; 405–842–7293.

- Oklahoma Parents Against Child Stealing, J. C. and Angela Kincaid, P.O. Box 2112, Bartlesville, OK 74005; 918–534–1489. Provides personal assistance to the custodial parent in location and recovery of missing children. Keeps informed about federal and state laws pertaining to missing children and makes these laws known to the victimized parents. Actively supports other organizations concerned with missing children.

- Operation Go-Home, Rev. Normal Johnston, P.O. Box 12, Westport, Ontario KOG 1X0; 613–273–2046. Canadian network for referrals from the missing child and/or parent.

- Operation Home Run, Steve Vaus, 4575 Ruffner St., San Diego, CA 92111; 800–647–7968.

- Parents Against Child Snatching, Kimberly Willis, 5554 Cobb Meadow, Norcross, GA 30093; 404–921–8526.

- Parents Against Child Stealing, Inc., Donna Hodge, P.O. Box 581, Coraopolis, PA 15108; 412–264–9025 and 412–526–5537. Offers advice, counseling, and guidance to the parents of abducted children. PACS helps to locate missing children and aids parents in their search. Can recommend other services—legal counsel, private detectives, and self-help.

- Parents Helping Parents, Rt. 1, Box 406D, Myakka City, FL 33551.

- Parents of Murdered Children, Charlotte Hullinger, 1739 Bella Vista, Cincinnati, OH 45327; 513–721–LOVE and 513–242–8025. Compassionate outreach program. A self-help support organization with groups for parents and other homicide survivors. Chapters are located throughout the United States.

- Roberta Jo Society, The, Robin Steely, 129 E. Main St., Chillicothe, OH 45601; 614–772–1781.
- Searching Parents Association, Sue Humphrey, P.O. Box 582, East Tawas, MI 48730; 517–362–7148.
- Edwin Shaw, IV, Inc., Sandy Shaw, 615 E. First Ave., Chadbourn, NC 28431; 919–654–5501. Can get information distributed through contacts in trucking industry. Sponsors Family Reunion Month.
- Single Parent, Ginny Nuta or Martha Mallardi, 7910 Woodmont Ave., Suite 1008, Bethesda, MD 20814; 301–654–8850.
- SLAM (Society's League Against Molestation), Patti Linebaugh, P.O. Box 102, Camarillo, CA 93010.
- Society for Young Victims, June Vlasaty, 29 Thurston Ave., Newport, RI 02840; 401–847–5083. First organization to lobby for national information centers. Licensed detective. Organizes search teams for police. Maintains scrapbooks and computerized statistics. Affiliate of Find-Me. Sponsors Family Reunion Month.
- Society for Young Victims, Massachusetts Chapter, John Soboleski, 5 Washington St., Manchester, MA 01944; 617–526–1080.
- Stolen Child Information Exchange, Barbara Freeman, 2523 Daphne Place, Fullerton, CA 92633.
- Margaret Strickland, 420 Milford Point Rd., Merritt Island, FL 32952; 305–452–8707. Author of *How To Deal With A Parental Kidnapping*. Copies may be obtained by sending $14 to Rainbow Books, P.O. Box 1069, Raven, FL 33471.
- Tania Murrell Missing Children Society, The, Mr. and Mrs. Jack Murrell, 9913–151 St., Edmonton, Alberta, T5P 1T2; 403–486–7777. Goals are to aid any way possible in the location of lost or missing children and to assist searching parents. Information recording, posters. Telephone tip line.
- Texas Child Search, Inc., Carolyn Huebner, P.O. Box 8122, San Antonio, TX 78028; 512–224–7939.
- Top Priority: Children, Teddy Kieley, P.O. Box 2161, Palm

Springs, CA 92263; 619–323–1559. Distributes free newsletter on children's issues. Working on the problems of missing children.

- 20 DB's Orange County Search and Rescue "National Kid Print" Program, Carol Stockdale, Founder, Executive Director of "National Kid Print," P.O. Box 5548, Buena Park, CA 90622; 714–983–0945 and 714–778–0375. Provides education program in child safety, using coloring book, brochures, video and slide presentations, and a fingerprinting program that is totally compatible with the FBI NCIC system. Supplies everything that is needed to establish a fingerprint and safety program or a chapter of "National Kid Print."

LISTING OF PICTURES

A possible means of reaching missing persons is through various publications that may be read by the victim, friends of the victim, or professional organizations. Success depends upon someone's connecting the information and the picture with the characteristics of the missing person. The following groups provide this service. Contact them for current fees if you choose to pursue this avenue of search.

- Child Find, Inc. (see page 114), is perhaps the largest provider of directories of missing children.
- American Federation of Police, 1100 NE 125th St., North Miami, FL 33161; 305–891–1700; 1000 Connecticut Ave NW, Suite 9, Washington, DC 20036; *National Crime Watch Magazine* is now part of *Police Times*. Sponsors Child-Guard Data Center and will provide free space for photos of missing children. Magazine has circulation of 21,000 police and sheriff agencies. Gerald S. Arenberg, Editor.
- Search, 560 Sylvan Avenue, Englewood Cliffs, NJ 07632; 201–567–4040. Publishes *National Runaway/Missing Persons Report* with photos and descriptions of missing people, mails it nationally to law enforcement officials at municipal, county, and state level, and to hospitals, social services, and transportation terminals.

NR/MPR includes medical histories, required medications, blood type, psychiatric background (if appropriate), work and recreation habits, normal style of dress, data on substance abuse, and so on.

DETECTIVES

The Clinkscales, founders of Find-Me, Inc., also provide a sample of detective listings that may be beneficial to searching parents. They advise using care in selecting a detective. Put financial arrangements in writing before continuing the process (see page 117).

- Aardwolfe Detectives, William J. Neal, #A4888, 17700 S. Western Ave., #52, Gardena, CA 90248; 213–324–7680. Has specialized service in missing persons, custody cases, and missing heirs. Their flat fee of $300 covers 10 manhours, 100 miles in mileage, and reward. Expenses are extra. Investigates factual information (clues) provided by client to determine the possibility of locating the missing person.

- Ambassador Investigations, Inc., Alice Byrne, 554 Argyle Road, Brooklyn, NY 11230; 212–282–1700. National low-cost detective service for locating missing persons. Free consultation.

- Angell Investigative Service, P.O. Box 1241, Dade City, FL 33525; 904–567–2909. Service is provided by a former law enforcement person.

- Chambers Investigations, Inc., Charles L. Chambers, PI, 606 49th St. W., Bradenton, FL 33529; 813–792–1107. Fully trained and experienced investigators. Currently involved in missing persons, very reasonable rates. Member of an investigator group that extends throughout the world that is known as the Worldwide Network of Reciprocal Agents.

- Criminal Investigations, Inc., Richard D. Thompson, P.O. Box 2596, Anniston, AL 36202; 205–237–9598. Retired federal special agent (DOD Criminal Investigator). Has more than twenty-three years of investigative experience, most having been in covert drug suppression efforts in Europe. Has highly skilled investigative service.

- Locators International, Harvey E. Morse, 1470 Gene St., Winter Park, FL 32789; 305–831–2000. Has more than twenty years of experience; expert on custodial matters, parental abductions, missing persons; works with legal profession and law enforcement.
- R. J. Perry Investigators, Inc., 2022 West Oakton St., Park Ridge, IL 60068; 312–696–0930. Licensed private detectives specializing in missing persons and "lost children."
- Quint and Associates, Lyle Quint, 430 Earle Lane, Montrose, CO 81401; 303–249–3387. Specializing in missing persons; very low rates for such cases. Computerized fingerprinting and identification system.
- Sentry Investigators, Sidney Schulman, 6010 Wilshire Blvd., Los Angeles, CA 90034; 213–939–7359. States that if missing person is not found in six months, fee will be refunded. A California-licensed private investigation firm. Worldwide service; founded in 1973.
- Lloyd Shulman, Mr. Keene, Tracer of Missing Persons, P.O. Box 17790F, Los Angeles, CA 90017; 213–380–2400. Finds missing relatives, adoptees, birth parents, old friends, and old sweethearts. Excellent success rate. More than twenty years' experience. Every inquiry given careful attention. State license.
- Southland Investigators, Charles Saunders, 3022 N. Hesperian St., Suite 201, Santa Ana, CA 92706; 714–543–3692. Specializing in locating children missing by parental or criminal kidnapping. "Our fees are affordable," they say.
- Whitney Investigations, Frank Military, P.O. Box 18000, Suite 212, Las Vegas, NV 89114; 702–798–8447. Devotes 10 percent of time to those who cannot afford services. More than thirteen years' experience in missing person cases.

Find-Me, Inc. reports that the following hotlines are operational:

- Metro-Help, Inc.: 808–972–6004 (Illinois), 800–621–4000 (Other states)

- Governor's Office for Volunteer Services: 800–382–3352 (Texas), 800–231–6946 (Other states)
- Runaway Assistance Program (RAP): 800–292–4517 (Michigan)

The Dee Scofield Awareness Program, Inc., reports that the following runaway hotline numbers are also available for parents and children.

- National Runaway Switchboard. 1–800–621–4000. (National will take messages from parents within Illinois at 1–800–972–6004.)
- Operation Peace of Mind (national). 1–800–231–6946.
- National Parents Anonymous Hotline. 1–800–421–0353.
- Child Abuse Hotline. 1–800–252–5400.

The National Fund for Runaway Children provides listings of runaway shelters nationwide. Write % Act Together, 1511 K Street NW, Suite 805, Washington, DC 20005.

These listed agencies and individuals have great concern for parents and children in need. They battle to educate the public and change the perception of child rights. If your needs are met through their efforts, please let them know. Your contribution to the cause will make a brighter tomorrow for all children.

Chapter 11

The People Behind
the Safety Organizations

Their stories are never easy to tell, but the personal accounts of the founders of several child safety organizations are so enlightening that they must be retold for parents everywhere.

The following is the history of Find-Me, Inc., as told by John and Louise Clinkscales, its founders.

Before the late 1970s, the phenomenon of missing persons was a mystery subject. Like cancer before an enlightened medical time, an affected family would suffer with relatively little support from the general public. The only ones outside the family who knew about a missing person were close friends and relatives who could offer no help, only sympathy. The public was generally unaware of the problem, and perception of the phenomenon of missing persons was primarily that of runaways.

It was in this environment that we became involved with the problem created by the disappearance of a family member. On January 27, 1976, our only son left LaGrange, Georgia, presumably to return to Auburn University in Alabama, about forty-five miles away. Kyle never arrived, and we soon learned that we had traveled back to the "dark ages."

At that time virtually all missing persons were perceived to be runaways. And runaways were generally thought to be escaping intolerable home conditions. Law enforcement officials had little or no interest. When we went to the Police Department to report our son missing, the information was written on a scrap of paper found on the counter. All that was asked was his name, age, Social Security number, type and color of his car, and its license number.

We soon learned that if there was anything to be done to try to solve the case of the disappearance of our son, we would have to do it. At first we were at a loss as to what to do. We felt as if we were in a vacuum. The public was so devoid of awareness of the problem that our own pastor offered no comment, yet there is no other emotional experience that can compare with it.

Our efforts to find Kyle have fallen into the following general phases: (1) offering a reward and depending upon regular law enforcement to solve the case; (2) getting publicity on the case; (3) getting some kind of national coverage; (4) writing about our experiences; and (5) getting a TV special devoted to missing persons.

Organizing a resource center was not one of the things we considered. At that time there was no known center for distributing information on the phenomenon. It was two or three years later before we even heard of such a group. We began reading everything we could find on the subject. Most of the articles were of a local nature. Fortunately, the company where John worked was conducting a customer survey that required subscribing to newspapers from all over the United States. This gave us access to many newspapers. Occasionally we would read of an agency that was devoted to the problem; generally the agency had been founded as a result of a disappearance and the inability of the family to find any aid.

As we progressed from one phase to another, our emphasis gradually changed from being solely concerned with our own case to the problem in general. It took us about five years to cover all the five phases of the foregoing list in our efforts. When we read of an agency working in the field of missing persons, we would write to it. But every such letter was returned, stamped "Moved, left no forwarding address," or some similar postal rejection.

Our manuscript became a book: Kyle's Story: Friday Never Came, The Search for Missing People. *In the final stages of the completion of* Kyle's Story, *we came up with the concept of Find-Me, Inc. (For* INDi-*viduals Missing Everywhere). We felt that a resource center was needed and that if no one else would come up with one, we would.*

In late 1980, we managed to get the address and telephone number of Julie Patz. From her we learned of about a half dozen agencies active in the field of missing persons. (Etan Patz, Julie's son, had disappeared, and she had been successful in obtaining information on the existence of those agencies.)

As our emphasis changed from that of our individual case to that of the problem in general, the public perception was also changing. Although the first public perception of the phenomenon was that of runaways, now a new element was capturing the public imagination—parental abduction.

The method of dispensing information to those who seek it is the ACTION booklet. We wanted a publication that we could send free to anyone. The publication was to give information, advice, and counseling.

ACTION is A Confederation To Inform Others Nationally. Its purposes are:

(1) to inform legislative personnel, news media, and the general public about the magnitude of the problem; (2) to act as a handbook for families who have someone missing; (3) to urge law makers to pass needed legislation; (4) to urge law enforcement personnel to give missing cases a higher priority; and (5) to urge the missing who may read the booklet to get in contact with their family even if they want to keep their whereabouts secret.

We receive requests for nearly 2000 copies of ACTION each year. It was never an objective of Find-Me, Inc., or of the ACTION booklet to print and distribute pictures of the missing. We felt that the likelihood of making an identification through the distribution method used for the ACTION booklet was so remote that it did not justify the expense and the space required to include pictures. We did not have the resources to pursue such a course. Rather, we wanted to give information directly to the families who requested it. We wanted to try to impress the size of the problem upon the media, the public, and all levels of the government.

As a result of the Etan Patz case, Representative Paul Simon (D–IL) became interested in the problem and decided to introduce legislation on the subject. His office could find no information on missing persons. Somewhere, someone advised his office that if anyone in the United States knew anything about missing persons, it was John and Louise Clinkscales. On January 19, 1981, we met with Marilyn McAdams, a staff member of the House of Representatives Select Subcommittee on Education, who was given the task of the actual drafting of the legislation for Representative

Simon. The ACTION booklet was included in the written testimony for the Missing Children Act.

Our activity got the attention of Robert Lamb, a writer for the Atlanta Journal–Constitution. *His story about our efforts was featured on the front page, and as a result we were invited to appear on the hour-long Cable News Network's "Freeman Reports." The program featured Kyle's case in particular and the overall problem in general. Appearing with us from the Washington Bureau was Representative Simon.*

About this time Senator Paula Hawkins (R–FL) also became interested in the problem of missing children. We were contacted by Jay Howell, who was drafting the legislation for Senator Hawkins.

Although the missing persons phenomenon has come from almost total public ignorance to the forefront of public concern within the past five or six years, the perception is really misleading. A careful analysis will indicate that a large portion of the activity concerning missing persons concerns parental kidnapping. Perhaps this is a result of the emphasis being placed by the media on that activity. The public responds in kind. When we appeared on the "Freeman Reports," all but two of the responses we received were about missing young adults (Kyle was twenty-two years old at the time of his disappearance). One of these concerned a four-year-old girl and the other concerned a sixty-five-year-old man.

There are many facets of the phenomenon of missing persons. The major ones are as follows: (1) abduction of the very young for the purposes of the abductor or to sell into illegal adoption channels; (2) brain washing by so-called religious cults; (3) child snatching by a divorced or separated parent from the other parent who has custody; (4) teens entrapped into prostitution or drug pushing who cannot or will not keep contact with family; (5) victims of an unknown murder; and (6) voluntary, with or without reason—teens running away from intolerable home conditions, adults escaping broken marriages, and the like.

Many of the agencies dispensing aid and information in the field of missing persons are "topical," that is, they work in certain phases only and will not accept requests from others if the person is over a certain age. Find-Me, Inc. is a general agency, accepting requests from anyone. Some of the topical agencies refer their rejections to Find-Me, Inc.

When the missing person is alive and is a teenager or older, the probability of his or her being found is remote if there are no clues left behind. About the only chance of locating the person is if he or she becomes involved in some kind of illegal activity. Thus, if contact is reestablished, it must originate with the missing person. For that reason Find-Me, Inc. had an original goal of getting the concept of Family Reunion Month established. Simply put, the concept for Family Reunion Month is for everyone who has not had contact with his or her family for the previous year (for any reason) to call, write, or visit the family during the period from Mother's Day to Father's Day.

Because of lack of funds, the Family Reunion Month idea was basically dormant until 1983. Then the proclamation was adopted by several states and many cities. In early May 1983, the resolution was introduced in the U. S. Senate by Senator Mack Mattingly (R–GA). For such a resolution to be taken up by the senate, it has to be co-sponsored by at least 25 percent (25) of the senators. This sponsorship was obtained, and the resolution passed the Senate in 1983.

The resolution was also introduced in the U. S. House of Representatives by Representative Richard Ray (D–GA). The House requires cosponsoring by at least 50 percent (218). We were told by several people in Washington that we could never get 50 percent of the representatives to sign on as co-sponsors. However, the minimum number was exceeded in May 1984.

When the resolution reached the White House for approval, President Reagan was so impressed with the concept that he invited us, through Senator Mattingly, to come to the White House to give us the pen he used to sign the resolution May 31, 1984. We went to the White House on June 26.

The real benefit of getting the resolution through Congress and signed by President Reagan is to make it easier to get publicity. Find-Me, Inc., will be making a major push to get publicity in future years. We know that the concept is working. We feel that the success will be in direct ratio to the publicity that can be generated.

The emphasis that Find-Me, Inc. put on the ACTION booklet is paying off. The feedback that we get indicates that it is considered as the "bible" on the missing persons phenomenon. We have received requests from TV and radio stations, newspapers, magazines, police departments, and family and youth organizations from all over the United States and many Canadian locations.

In the evolution of the missing persons phenomenon to the current level of awareness, the ACTION booklet has become vitally important in parental abductions and of secondary importance in other abductions involving child abuse. Only Find-Me, Inc. and a few other agencies are trying to maintain an equitable balance to represent all facets adequately. Awareness of missing persons will not be pervasive in our society until this is done.

We have made an impact on the problem, as is proven in the areas in which we participate. Although the National Center for Missing and Exploited Children is heavily weighted to children, John was selected to be a director. We were invited to address the Children and Youth Committee of the American Legion at their executive meeting on May 7, 1984, in Indianapolis. We get many requests from the media in various cities who think that Kyle's case involved a very young person. Some lose interest when they learn otherwise, but others feature the story.

In promoting the awareness of the phenomenon we have appeared on TV in many cities. We were included briefly in ABC-TV News and have been mentioned in many national publications and other newspapers.

Find-Me, Inc., has two basic goals: (1) to make the public aware of all the elements of the missing person phenomenon, and (2) to reach the missing without violating their right to privacy.

By making the public aware of all the facets of the phenomenon of missing persons, perhaps many disappearances or abductions could be prevented. A case that does not happen does not have to be solved. By taking all reasonable precautionary measures, we may prevent many of the young from being abducted. Running away is the response to a problem, real or imaginary. Spotting such a problem in its formative stage may lead to a solution other than running away. Abduction and foul play are results of opportunity. The right to privacy usually can be maintained without the total severance of family ties.

Even if these goals are reached, the phenomenon of missing persons will not be totally eliminated. But it no longer will be an epidemic.

The following is the history of The Dee Scofield Awareness Program, Inc., written by Betty DiNova, its executive director.

Until the mid-1970s, the only kidnapping commonly known to most Americans was that of the Lindbergh baby in 1932. At least, that's the only one that came readily to my mind when I first learned that my husband's twelve-year-old niece, Dee Scofield, had vanished from a shopping center in Ocala, Florida, on July 22, 1976.

Dee disappeared about two o'clock on a Thursday afternoon, but the news didn't filter down to us in Tampa until Saturday morning, two days later. Then the report by phone was third-hand and not too accurate.

"It's my brother Gus in Ohio," Vince whispered while still listening.

During the silence I watched with growing curiosity as my husband's genial smile changed into a worried frown. I was shocked by his next words.

"Kidnapped?" Vince echoed. "One of Toni's boys, you say?"

Toni was Vince's niece. Toni and her husband and two boys, aged seven and nine, were sharing a double-wide trailer with Lena and Joe Scofield and their two youngest children, twelve-year-old Dee-Dee and fifteen-year-old "Little Joe." They lived on a 40-acre tract of uncleared wilderness in Citra, Florida, twenty-six miles outside Ocala.

A call to Lena, Vince's sister, revealed that it was not one of Toni's boys but Lena's Dee-Dee who was missing. I remember thinking, how strange! I had always thought, on the basis of the Lindbergh kidnapping, that only small children were kidnapped and that the motive was always ransom.

The Scofields were not rich. Ten months previously they had moved from Hilliard, Ohio, to the wilderness site in Florida because they loved the state and because two of their three married daughters were already living there. Joe and Lena had bought a small barbecue stand in the rural Florida area and were barely eking out a living from the family-operated venture.

The day before Dee vanished, Joe and Little Joe had taken the day off to go fishing together. On Thursday, July 22, it was Lena and Dee's turn for a day off. They chose a movie for their recreation. First Lena stopped at the Florida Highway Patrol office at one corner of a shopping center in Ocala to take a written driver's test to get her Florida license. Before Lena went inside, Dee pleaded with her to let her go to the J. M Fields Department Store at the other end of the shopping center to buy Little Joe a birthday present and exchange a pair of sandals. This would save time so they wouldn't be late for the movie.

When Lena finished her driver's test and Dee had not returned, she went to the Fields store, but Dee wasn't there. Lena decided she must have missed her somehow along the way, but when she got back to the Highway Patrol office, Dee wasn't there either. Lena became concerned, and a kind patrolman, Lt. Bob Howard, helped her to search the shopping center more thoroughly. Maybe Dee had stopped in another store along the way. Lena began to panic when it was discovered that Dee had bought a watch band for Little Joe and had exchanged the sandals, but no one had seen her leave the store and no one in or around the other stores had seen her.

The Ocala police were notified, but according to department policy there was a twenty-four-hour waiting period before they could search. This first lesson in police procedures was frustrating, but the Scofields were law-abiding citizens who trusted and respected authority, so they accepted this policy as a matter of course and waited anxiously at home by the phone.

By the time Vince called them on Saturday morning, they seemed confident that the search was in good hands. An All Points Bulletin (APB) had been put out on Dee, all the news media had been informed, and even the FBI was in on the search. So the Scofields believed. But much later on we would learn that the FBI never assumes jurisdiction of any case; they "monitor" cases to determine when it would be appropriate for them to investigate. They investigate only out-of-state sightings or ransom demands, and they do not investigate at all unless asked to do so by jurisdictional police.

But at that time we, like the Scofields and countless other searching parents, assumed that all the authorities were doing everything possible to find Dee. Nevertheless, her disappearance was a sobering thought that stayed with us.

The first time I saw this shy, reserved child was on a visit to Ohio when she was not yet two. I was a camera buff, and small children were my favorite subjects. Dee-Dee reluctantly posed for me, in the security of her brother Joe's presence. During the next ten years, I saw her only a handful of times—once at a family wedding in Columbus and several times when the Scofields visited Florida. I now prize the photos I took of her on these occasions. When she was eight, Dee visited Tampa and became especially dear to me. My mother had died about ten weeks previously, and as the Scofields were gathered outside our home in the late dusk bidding us farewell, Dee thrust something into my hand when I kissed her. After they left, I found that the small memento was a tiny red book of Bible verses that I assumed was meant to comfort me in my loss. Perhaps, however, Dee was simply demonstrating her emerging Catholic faith. I may never know why she gave me the little book. I know only how much I cherish it.

Two hours after Dee's disappearance she was allegedly seen at a convenience store on the edge of the Ocala National Forest. If the twenty-four-hour waiting period had not been observed, this sighting could possibly have been followed up and might have culminated in Dee's safe recovery.

Three days after Dee's disappearance she was allegedly seen by a twelve-year-old classmate at a crossroads outside Ocala. Looking out the window of a "hippie"-type van, Dee was mouthing the word, "Help." This was not reported until twelve hours after it occurred, and the police gave very little credibility to the story. They did little more than keep an eye out within the city limits for a van meeting the schoolgirl's description of the suspect vehicle.

For the next two weeks there were hopeful signs that Dee might be with a man who liked children. His family had moved to the outskirts of Tampa the weekend before Dee disappeared, before his being transferred to the Tampa area where Dee was allegedly seen on three occasions. But when Joe Scofield came to Tampa to interview the lady who had seen Dee, she retracted her story and said she could not be sure it was Dee she had seen.

The relative complacency we all felt because of the numerous local sightings was suddenly shattered on Sunday morning, August 8, when the Scofields called from Ocala to report that they had just received a call from a family vacationing in the north. They said they had seen a girl resembling Dee being pushed into a car by a black man in front of a Holiday Inn motel in Indianapolis, Indiana. The bumper sticker on the car read "Blacks hate whites." The caller was a girl in her early twenties who had seen Dee's poster when she had passed through Ocala on her way north. It was later learned that she had recently been released from a mental hospital, so her story was also discredited by police.

In the meantime, we learned a second lesson in police procedures: It is next to impossible to get help from a police agency on a weekend. *The jurisdictional investigator in charge of Dee's case in Ocala was unavailable, and the officer on duty said he had no authority to call Indianapolis. The Scofields had been on their way to church when the call came. Because they could get no help from their own police, they left the sighting in our hands to be checked out by Tampa police and the Hillsborough County Sheriff's Department, both of which had been involved in the Tampa sightings of Dee. But we hit a snag here also and learned our third lesson in police politics:* Nonjurisdictional police cannot act without a direct request from the jurisdictional police. *We got a similar response from the local FBI office. The agent on duty said his office would report it to his supervisor in Jacksonville the next day, but he doubted that the FBI would get involved. It was not until 1982, six years later, that we came to realize that the FBI could not act without a request from jurisdictional police.*

Failing all else, we called the Indianapolis Police Department ourselves and were again told that they were not supposed to act without a request from jurisdictional police. However, in this case the police officer, a Mrs. Marcy, agreed to check it out for us anyway. The caller had allegedly gotten the name of the black man from the motel register, but when Mrs. Marcy checked with all the Holiday Inns in the city, none of them could find a recent registration under that name.

The Indianapolis experience, coupled with previous irregularities in the local investigation that we had accepted as police policy or as an understandable mistake, began to open our eyes to the fact that there really wasn't much of an official effort being made to find Dee. For instance, when Marilyn A. Greene, a founder of the American Rescue Dog Association, Albany, New York, offered the use of her search dogs to look for Dee in the dense expanse of the Ocala National Forest, Joe Scofield turned the offer over to the jurisdictional police for action . . . and none was taken. At that point the Scofields still trusted the judgment of the police and thus accepted their decision to decline this valuable opportunity as being in Dee's best interests. We were later to learn from this a fourth lesson: Police pride often keeps many police departments from accepting outside help of any kind, even from other police agencies.

Initially, when the Scofields were told that an APB had been issued on Dee, it was assumed that police agencies everywhere would be looking for her when they got the news of her disappearance. But a week later, when we contacted the Tampa and Hillsborough police officials with regard to the Tampa sightings, they were both totally unaware of the case. This was a pattern we were later to learn was standard throughout the United States, teaching us our fifth lesson: Unless there is reason to believe that a particular missing person is in their specific area, police routinely disregard APBs and flyers about them. *We would also learn later that the news media operate on this same premise.* Unless there is a local connection or a sensational angle, there is no coverage by the local media.

By September 1976, less than two months after Dee's disappearance, we had learned enough to know that thousands of American children were missing and little was being done to find them. This was a challenge to me personally because I have a special love for children. I was never able to have any of my own, so everyone else's seemed to become important to me. I also despise injustice, so I spent a lot of idle hours pondering what could be done. I began filling a scrapbook with newspaper clippings about other missing child cases.

At that time my daughter-in-law, Ivana DiNova (wife of Vince's son, Tony) lived in the next block from us. When we were together, Dee was an inevitable topic of conversation, and we would ask ourselves the question, Why Dee? I pondered that question each night when I went to bed and each morning when I woke up, and in the peaceful silence of those private moments my imagination toyed with some answers.

We had learned from the mail the Scofields received in response to the initial Associated Press release about Dee that there were many other parents throughout the country whose children had vanished and were still missing. We had no idea how many there might be, but we did know that all those who had written had similar experiences with their police. To awaken America to this problem and seek help in correcting it would take a mammoth effort. That brought the first answer . . . Dee's family was large. Not only did she have three married sisters, but she had seven aunts and uncles and numerous cousins. Many of them had small children of their own, and they were scattered over five far-flung states: California, Michigan, Virginia, Ohio, and Florida.

A second answer came from my own career experience. I knew how to prepare news releases and had been instrumental in getting the initial AP release on Dee's disappearance published. These were all elements that could be used to spread the word to the American people. My thirty collective years of executive secretarial experience for top echelon officials and administrators would also help. Now we needed to be armed with facts.

Ivana went with me to our local police department where we obtained some statistics and police viewpoints. She belonged to a local Catholic parish that had just instituted a church newspaper. So she wrote an article about Dee's disappearance, including local statistics on missing children, and asked the readers to "Help Start a Miracle" by becoming involved. That was the beginning of the Dee Scofield Awareness Program. The article was distributed to family members in other states, and most of them were able to get the article, or a condensed version of it, published in their church *newspapers or bulletins. This generated more letters, which became the start of the Dee Program's files.*

We sent out our first news release on Dee's thirteenth birthday, January 8, 1977, and followed it up with another on the anniversary of her disappearance, July 22, 1977. However, except for radio coverage, media response consisted of TV and newspaper interviews with Joe and Lena Scofield and no mention of the Dee Program, even though our purpose in sending out the releases had been to let other searching parents know we existed to help them also.

Discouraged, we did not send out a release on Dee's fourteenth birthday, but I continued to gather newspaper clippings for our missing child scrapbooks, filing them by state. I then fed the information, manually, from the clippings into statistics books that were also set up by state. Then an unexpected thing happened to encourage us and rejuvenate our fledgling organization.

Rita and Fred Reker, who were among the parents who had written the Scofields when Dee disappeared, were planning a trip from St. Cloud, Minnesota, to Florida and would stop to see the Scofields in Citra. Joe and Lena set up a meeting at their home to coincide with this visit of the Rekers and their four remaining children. Their daughters, Mary and Susan, aged fifteen and twelve, had vanished in September 1974 after walking to a shopping center near their home. They were missing nearly a month before their bodies were found at an abandoned quarry outside St. Cloud. Florida family members, other parents of missing and murdered children, and Orlando reporters were invited to the meeting. It was a memorable occasion that resulted in the incorporation of the organization. Rita Reker, Ivana, and I were the original directors. We reinstituted our news releases on July 22, 1978. In October 1978 we signed incorporation papers, gaining official corporate status as of January 16, 1979. Recognition by the IRS as a tax-exempt, nonprofit organization did not come until February 1982 after nearly a year of grappling with government red tape.

Up to this point our main focus had been on compiling the scrapbooks and statistics. What little media coverage we received brought in a few small donations, but the first real breakthrough in the media came in October 1980 from an AP release generated by Stanley and Julie Patz. They were the parents of six-year-old Etan Patz who had been missing from their Manhattan home since May 25, 1979. In the article they called for a national clearinghouse to find all missing children. We were one of eight agencies already in existence that responded to this plea, and Julie Patz put us all in touch with each other so that we could coordinate our efforts.

The 1980 AP release also caught the eye of Congressman Paul Simon, D–IL, who began researching the problem and subsequently introduced the first Missing Children Act into the U.S. House of Representatives. We were able to provide his office with the only available statistics on the subject at the time—a report on 417 cases from our scrapbooks. Later, Senator Paula Hawkins, R–FL, introduced an improved Missing Children Act in the U.S. Senate. It was subsequently passed and signed into law by President Ronald Reagan on October 12, 1982.

However, what really triggered the momentum for passage of this legislation was the bizarre case of another six-year-old boy who disappeared on July 27, 1981, and whose severed head was found two weeks later near a canal more than 100 miles away. Nearly all Americans are now familiar with the story of Adam Walsh of Hollywood, Florida, who was the inspiration for the TV movie, "Adam," which was initially aired on October 10, 1983. A roll call at the end of the movie, showing photos of fifty-five currently missing children, was credited with locating eleven of the children. The movie was again aired on April 30, 1984, with a different set of photos that netted additional recoveries. When the movie was aired overseas in Wales with the first set of photos in May 1984, two boys who had been kidnapped from Massachusetts in 1982 by their noncustodial father were recognized and reported to the show's producers, resulting in their subsequent recovery by their mother.

Credit for instituting photo publicity as a means of locating missing children must go to the magazine publishers who used photos of missing children to illustrate the early articles on this subject in the spring of 1981. To our knowledge, the first recovery was that of James Kennedy, a parentally kidnapped boy whose photo appeared in the April 1981 issue of the Ladies' Home Journal.

National recognition of the Dee Program came when the Reader's Digest *published a photo of Wavie Batson, a missing Florida teenager whose parents were registered with us. We received more than sixty sightings from that one photo in the July 1982 issue, but it was the tenth sighting call that resulted in Wavie's recovery after an absence of two and a half years. The* Reader's Digest *followed this up with a story about her recovery in their November 1982 issue and included six more photos from our files. We began to receive not only sightings of the children but inquiries from* concerned citizens on how they could get involved. It also brought us requests for help from searching parents.

Although we started with a simple awareness program in 1976, we now have a threefold commitment to Americans: (1) to provide search guidance and compassionate support to families of vanished children (we do not handle parental kidnaps); (2) to obtain better laws, simplified jurisdictional channels and improved investigations; and (3) to create public awareness and ensure child safety through awareness projects, photo exhibits, and educational literature. Our program also includes resource lists of other agencies, books, safety programs, and prevention and identification materials. There is no charge for our services or literature.

Today is the eighth anniversary of Dee's disappearance, and it is with a heavy heart that I reflect on those eight years. Now, in the peaceful silence of my private moments with God each morning and evening, I ponder how wonderful it would be if Dee were here to see the results of her sacrifice.

In 1979 Ivana moved to Brandon, Florida, twenty miles east of our headquarters in Tampa, and became inactive in our program. Then media attention began bringing in requests for our assistance. She became our spokesperson while I continued to handle all written material and correspondence. In March 1982 Ivana left the Dee Program and started the Missing Children Help Center in Brandon.

In its eight years of existence, the Dee Program has become an established and well-respected segment of a national network of missing child agencies throughout the United States. It is recognized as a valid source of information on missing child issues, being active in national projects related to missing children and endorsing programs and products designed for the safety, protection, and identification of children.

The question "Why Dee?" may have been answered by the Dee Program's contributions to the national effort on behalf of missing children and their families, but the question of what happened to Dee has yet to be answered.

The Bible says, "To every thing there is a season, and a time to every purpose under the heaven [Ecclesiastes 3:1]. Lena Scofield reflected her faith in this promise in a TV interview for Missing Children Day, 1983. When asked what she thought had happened to Dee, she replied with poignant simplicity and quiet courage, "I don't know, but I'm sure I'll get my answer some day."

Chapter 12

National Recognition

The efforts of the families of missing and murdered children turned national recognition to the problem of the molested and vanished child. One of the first child victims to obtain nationwide public attention was six-year-old Adam Walsh, who was abducted and murdered in 1981. The death of this bright-eyed little boy with the endearing toothless grin propelled his parents into the midst of an uninformed society. Not willing to let their child become another forgotten statistic, they joined energies to inform the nation about the incredible problem of crimes against children. Willing to give wholeheartedly of their time, John and Reve Walsh talked to anyone who would listen. They spent frustrating years carving a path through the wilderness of public ignorance of child-related crimes.

Then through their grief came the first sense of public awareness, spurred by a television movie depicting the tragedy of their son's death. "Adam" awakened the world to the deadly problems parents in this nation face daily. The movie, first aired in fall 1983, was followed by a display of the pictures of some missing children, with the Walsh family reading their names.

Because Florida is the Walshes' home state, they concentrated a great deal of their work there, beginning the Adam Walsh Child Resource Center in Fort Lauderdale. Hence, Florida has become a model state for child legislation. This heightened state awareness spread to a nationwide level as John and Reve became involved in the work that had changed the course of their lives. Through their persistence and interaction with government officials and other parents of missing children, they championed the Missing Children's Act that was passed in 1982. The act established a way to include data on missing children in the FBI national crime computer. It also provided for a clearinghouse on unidentified bodies. This rudimentary genesis led to the Missing Children's Assistance Act, which provides $10 million for three years for grants to be used to maintain a national resource center for children. The act covers the cost of a national hotline for reports on missing children and a periodic incidence study to collect data on missing children. The National Center for Missing and Exploited Children is the end result of this act.

John Walsh, who serves as one of the center's special advisors, continues to spread his urgent message regarding child rights to each state in the nation. He addresses state leaders by introducing a model packet of legislation covering the rights of children. In addition, he has been responsible for supporting VICAP (Violent Crimes Apprehension Program). This computerized tracking system is needed for the identification and arrest of mass murderers.

Undaunted by bureaucratic stalling and political strategies, these parents have become a new breed of missionaries. Transformed from an average mother and father into evangelists for children's rights, they have worked a special kind of miracle. They are pioneer parents.

THE NATIONAL CENTER
FOR MISSING AND EXPLOITED CHILDREN

An inventive new organization, The National Center for Missing and Exploited Children, opened its doors in 1984 to provide services that include the following:

- A division to deal with the many problems associated with missing children that offers search guidelines and a national directory of nonprofit organizations ready to aid parents.
- A division on exploited children that gives aid and training to law enforcement agencies.
- A division of public awareness and education that includes training, prevention, and coordination among involved federal and local groups.
- A toll-free, hotline for the public to report information about missing children: 1–800–843–5678. For Alaska and Hawaii, call 1–202–634–9836.

FLORIDA STATUTES THAT CAN BE INCORPORATED BY ALL STATES

The Adam Walsh Child Resource Center furnished the following information on statutes that may be implemented by other states:

- A state can begin a computer system that will track a vanished child by personal characteristics.
- A state can begin an official newsletter for police departments and schools that will include information about vanished children with a requirement that authorities be notified when a youngster is identified from the information.
- A state can bypass the twenty-four- to forty-eight-hour period of waiting before the police list the child with the NCIC. States can also ensure that police departments in the vicinity of the place where the child vanished have needed information.
- A state can begin a data center on vanished children that will give information concerning:
  - The availability of aids to help find vanished children
  - Information and pictures of vanished children to be sent to police departments and news media
  - Education for the public and all police departments concern-

ing such matters as fingerprinting and other services offered by the data center
- Proper methods of managing situations involving vanished children

LAWS SUGGESTED FOR ALL STATES

The following are some types of laws suggested for all states:

- Free background FBI and NCIC reports on any person involved in a children's or young persons' group or within the education system. This includes a stated requirement of fingerprinting for any individual wishing to receive licensing or certification.
- Harsh punishment for sentenced pedophiles to prevent them from being tried according to previously used measures.
- The adoption of guidelines that mandate absentee reporting of children by schools.
- The notification of all sexually assaulted persons concerning the precise time their assailants will be freed from jail.
- The adoption of guidelines needed to begin fingerprint centers for storage purposes.
- The adoption of guidelines to require schools to get needed identification on new pupils, as well as school documents.

These remarkable strides and valuable suggestions made in the area of children's legislation are increasing the level of safety awareness throughout the nation. Like a multitude of raindrops that join to create enormous oceans, the small strides of concerned parents will form a unified bond of perpetual care to surround their young.

A parent's idea of maximizing children's safety comes into focus with fingerprinting, school absentee reporting, and safety organizations. These helpful programs can be initiated indi-

vidually and taken into the community for expanded participation.

FINGERPRINTING

Fingerprinting is not a safety assurance but, rather, a precautionary measure. Police can get fingerprints in the child's original location of disappearance and send them to the NCIC for
further reference. Fingerprinting is becoming a widely accepted
practice in many communities because it can be incorporated
into civic projects and school programs.

The Dee Scofield Awareness Program suggests that parents
select an organization, such as the Parent Teacher Association of
their child's school, to be an official volunteer sponsor. Other
groups within a community may also be interested in providing
this type of service. Local police departments may be able to give
valuable leads that will be helpful in locating interested persons.
The police department may be encouraged by parents to set up
their own fingerprinting program at a public place. Find-Me,
Inc., reports that a local sheriff can obtain fingerprint cards
from the National Sheriff's Association, Suite 320, 1250 Connecticut Avenue, Washington, DC 20036. The first 500 cards ordered are free.

Once a sponsoring organization is found, a public relations
representative from the sheriff's or police departments can be
asked to help oversee the project. They can give special training
seminars to the core of volunteers and can be encouraged to loan
kits needed to take fingerprints.

One person from the volunteer group should be trained to
explain the procedure to the children so that the experience will
be a positive one. Volunteers may assist in many ways, including
marking sign-up sheets, keeping order, performing the actual
process of fingerprinting, filling out cards, cleaning up, and
giving cards to parents.

Parents should know that no one, including the police or

sponsors of the organization, will be allowed to keep the fingerprint cards on file. Only the child's guardian will have access to the fingerprints, which the guardian should keep in the child's personal file folder. The Dee Scofield Awareness Program will provide parents with helpful guidelines for the procedure if requested. The American Federation of Police sponsors a project called Child Guard. They offer a parents' prevention manual that is available on request. The manual contains suggested fingerprint forms as well as other vital data space.

SCHOOL ABSENTEE REPORTING

Child safety organizations agree that schools should make reporting absentees part of the daily schedule to warn parents if their children do not report to class. This vital program can be a lifesaver for a child who is abducted on the way to school. A missing persons report can immediately be made by parents and a search begun if this program is established. Without such a valuable warning, parents might not be aware for an entire school day that their child is missing. Crimes against children are becoming so prevalent that there is a definite need for action on the part of every school.

Several systems of absentee reporting are currently being used. The first requires voluntary participation of parents whose children attend the school. Parents are notified when they are required to take class reports on absentee children. During a specified hour, the volunteers make rounds of each classroom. Teachers provide information on all children who are missing from class, writing the names on the volunteers' absentee forms. The volunteer returns to the office and notifies the parents of all missing children on the list. Excuses for absences should be noted on the absentee form. If a parent is surprised that a child is not in class, direction should be given to aid the parent. A list of helpful organizations should be kept in the office for parents who need scarch information.

Junior and senior high schools should require teachers to report missing pupils at the beginning of each class period to cover students who skip classes during the day. Students from the classroom can deliver absentee reports to the office. All reports should be made in ink to prevent erasure. Students who travel by bus and who are late should be listed on separate forms that are kept in class.

The second method of absentee reporting involves volunteer students from each class. After rolls are called, two students from each class, called runners, take the reports to the office. The process for notifying parents of a missing child is left to the school office personnel. This runner system has proved slightly more effective than the volunteer method because of the inconsistency of parents in being available as scheduled.

However, in both cases the final report on missing children should be given to the principal, who, if necessary, can coordinate a schoolground search to help police and the families of children who disappear on their way to school.

PARENT SAFETY CLUB

Groups of concerned parents are organizing to protect the interests of children in their communities. Some organize for specific purposes, such as shutting down pornography that is seeping into town. Others band together to form teams of "patrol parents" who diligently assist in patroling areas where children walk to school. They can be seen on any school morning walking children across streets or helping little ones who become frightened. Their presence creates a deterrent to crime against children. The Dee Scofield Awareness Program reports that 15 percent of all child disappearances occur while the child is walking or biking between home, school, or other places of activity such as shopping centers.

Parent Safety Clubs are effective groups capable of reducing injustices toward children through their consistent effort and evaluation of problems. Parents and grandparents who are interested in starting safety clubs may wish to use the following list of helpful guidelines.

1. Organize a meeting date for the core group of interested parents.
2. Parents should appoint leaders and set meeting dates during their first gathering. A suggested format for the organizational meeting should include the following:
   - A parent leader to welcome the group.
   - Appoint a speaker, possibly from the field of law enforcement, or a school official. The speaker can be assigned a brief talk in which he or she must point out problem areas in child safety and encourage parents to form into an action group.
   - Recognition of appointed leaders, goal discussion, and meeting dates.
   - Secretary appointed to take names, phone numbers, and addresses of all participants.
   - Date for next meeting.
   - Refreshments.
   - Handouts from help groups such as the Dee Scofield Awareness Program. The Dee Scofield Awareness Program offers excellent guidelines for parent organizations. Some groups prefer to set requirements for group membership in order to be certain that they don't attract child molesters. These ideas should be thoroughly discussed by leaders before the organizational meeting.
   - SLAM (Society's League Against Molestation) can be asked by leaders for effective guidelines.
3. Advertise the program on the radio and in the newspaper.

ALTERNATIVES IN TEACHING SAFETY

Creative alternatives in teaching safety are used by many groups who realize that it may take extra effort to capture a child's attention. Two of the most outstanding programs involve the use of puppets and robots.

OPD2: The Robot with a Heart

The newest member of the Orlando, Florida, Police Department is named OPD2 and is still gaining popularity and success as he rolls through classrooms and makes appearances. This space-age, five-foot, four-inch, 197-pound robot is a contemporary safety trainer, capable of holding any child's attention as he teaches the vital basics of safety.

Purchased by $14,750 of confiscated drug money, OPD2 is watched after by full-time friend and police officer, Joseph Bongiorno. According to the man behind the machine, the Orlando Police Department was the first in the country to buy a robot and use it in a full-time capacity for teaching child safety. "It's almost impossible to measure the worth of a safety deterrent before a crime occurs. But there might be hundreds of children we have saved," says Bongiorno.

OPD2, who is dressed in the Orlando police uniform, has a video screen in his chest to allow children to view safety films. Although the robot appears to be in complete control of training sessions, it is really Joseph Bongiorno who operates him at a distance.

Together, the pair of trainers have spread the teachings of child safety in such locations as Disneyworld, the Tangerine Bowl, nursery schools, elementary schools, and civic clubs. Calls come in from across the nation requesting OPD2 to make appearances. But he declines, happily staying near home while teaching, saving lives, and making thousands of new friends.

The McGruff Elementary School Puppet Program

A popular child safety program presented by Puppet Productions of San Diego, California, in cooperation with the national crime prevention and advertising councils, is bringing a furry, trench-coated dog named McGruff into elementary school classrooms.

McGruff, whose motto is "Take a bite out of crime," brings his special crew of puppet friends to help teachers train children about safety. The program, which is designed to be a continual learning experience, costs approximately $65 per classroom. Presented by schoolroom teachers for fifteen minutes a week during the school year, the puppets teach memorable lessons by performing along with an audio cassette.

In addition to teaching about all types of childhood dangers, McGruff became a national celebrity in the fall of 1984 when his picture was released on millions of United States postal stamps.

Schools and parents interested in learning more about the McGruff safety programs may write Bill Hawes, McGruff Elementary School Program, P.O. Box 82008, San Diego, CA 92138. Or call toll-free 1-800-854-2151.

A Final Word

Visualizing the solution to the overwhelming issues of child molestation is much like searching for a patch of blue in a sky full of thunderclouds. Turbulent reminders, such as the increasing number of child victims, are daily shadows falling across our path. They signify with shocking clarity that we must become better equipped to resolve the burdensome flood of crimes against our young.

The one consistent element in the pattern of such crimes is the lack of comprehensive statistics. Everyone quotes them, whether in a broad or specific sense, but few people are sure where they originate. Dramatic and misleading statements supposedly based on statistics quickly capture public attention and lend an aura of authority to those persons who offer the information.

One of the most common statements implies that a sexually abused child might grow up to be a child molester. It is rare to see actual statistics accompanying this statement because nationwide figures are not available to verify the claim. The hazard of this particular statement is unmistakable. It creates an ongoing victimization of the innocent, who must bear the stigma of molestation for a lifetime. In contrast, it would be refreshing to be reminded that a great number of adults who were sexually abused as children now work in related fields to prevent such injustices.

A former child sexual assault victim and mother of three, shares her insight with parents:

I feel that one of the biggest problems for parents is that we are overrun with great numbers of people who profess to be experts in the field of child sexual abuse. Our greatest hint to their degree of expertise should be that they have only a tiny bit of knowledge to tell us why these things happen. And they can't tell us what to do to stop these abuses or how to effectively help families and children who have had this type of trauma in their lives. It seems that children have so few rights that they are often held accountable for the crime enacted against them. In my opinion, many times the criminal is let go to sexually abuse again, because he is protected by the law.

I'm not afraid to report that I was a victim of sexual abuse as a child. I know of others who experienced similar abuses, but they are afraid to come forward. People have a tendency to say a grown person who was molested as a child will become a child molester. Frankly, nothing could be farther from the truth. I know a number of people who had terrible childhood molestation experiences, but they all have great respect and love for children. They would never do anything to harm a child. Several of them now work in rape crisis centers and do a tremendous job helping women and children.

Parents often ask me to tell them the best way to protect their child. One of the really important things that we must do is to teach our children the names of sexual organs and their functions. As parents, we often give ridiculous nicknames to body parts. By doing this we instill a sense of embarrassment in our children. Kids might begin to think that sex and sexual abuse are subjects to avoid talking about. Then if they have questions, they will go to someone else for the answers. Eventually a child will learn the real names for her sexual organs. When she does, don't you think she will wonder why everyone made such a big fuss and refused to tell her the truth?

But, on the other hand, if a child's questions are answered and she has a workable understanding of sex, everything else will fall into line. Suddenly, she can begin to understand what abuse of her body might mean.

When I was a child, no one taught me that there is a bad way to be touched.

If I had known that one thing, it would have saved me terrible suffering. I thought I had to obey all adults because they were my elders. I was never taught to use my judgment about whom to obey. Somehow it seemed that children had no rights. Only adults were allowed that privilege. I feel that the wrong set of instructions and signals were given to me as a child.

Parents often make these types of mistake. We end up victimizing our children by not teaching them what they need to know to survive in this world. We should let them know they are as important as adults. By listening to them and respecting any complaints of abuse, we will make life a lot harder for child molesters and easier for children.

Most children don't have explicit sexual knowledge. So when they describe an act of molestation or rape, it makes sense to listen. How would a child know what a rape was like if she weren't raped herself? How could a child describe a molestation if he weren't the victim of such an abuse?

Children rarely lie about being sexually abused. Parents should know that it takes a lot of courage for a child to admit he or she was raped or molested. If a parent refuses to listen and help the child, a vital part of that relationship can be damaged. Not to mention the fact that a child might become a continual target for the molester.

The last thing a child needs to hear is that her attacker is a poor, sick thing. In the first place, I don't believe child molesters are sick. What they do to children is strictly a matter of choice. If you could be present to see a child sexually abused, I doubt if you could talk yourself into thinking the molester is a poor, sick reject of society. The "sick" idea is a plea molesters use to defend themselves and to gain sympathy.

In my opinion our society and laws provoke crimes against children because we refuse to protect them legally. We often allow child abductors, rapists, and molesters the freedom to walk away from their crimes without any punishment.

The Adam Walsh Foundation gives an award called the Cracked Gavel. The award says that it's for judges who let molesters go without punishment. It says that a national study shows that each child molester is responsible for molesting an average of sixty-eight children. And another report stated that 75 percent of imprisoned molesters had had at least one prior conviction for sexual assault of a child. Isn't that incredible? These criminals repeat their offense on as many kids as society allows them.

It's been predicted that by 1990 something like 80 percent of all children under age six will have mothers who work. That adds a lot of worry because these kids will be in nursery schools. We have all felt the shockwave from some of these daycare centers that have sexually abused kids. I'd say it's going to be up to parents to push city and state governments into passing strict laws and providing daycare supervision to protect children. We will all need to keep an eye on the legislators, judges, and city officials who are responsible for putting these laws into action.

Bibliography

ABC News 20/20 transcript. "The Lures of Death," Martin Clancy, producer, Tom Jarriel, correspondent, Show #410, March 8, 1984, pp. 2–6.

Ambrosino, Lillian. "Runaways," Boston *Beacon Press,* 1971.

Armstrong, Louise. *Kiss Daddy Goodnight: A Speakout on Incest.* Hawthorne Books, N.Y. 1978.

Baker, David C. "The Sexploitation of Children in Pornography and Prostitution," *Pepperdine Law Review,* Vol. 5, p. 814, 1978.

Barry, Robert J. "Incest: The Last Taboo." FBI Law Enforcement Bulletin, Office of Congressional and Public Affairs, Washington, D.C., January 1984, pp. 2–9.

Betcher, Mary. "Special Program For Kids, San Diego County Sheriff's Department Develops Child Safety Program." *The Police Chief.* March 1981, pp. 24–25.

Bete, Channing L. Co., Inc. "What Everyone Should Know About the Sexual Abuse of Children," Scripto graphic booklet. South Deerfield, Mass., 1976.

Bongiorno, Joseph, interview. "OPD2—The Robot With a Heart." Orlando, Fla. Police Department, September, 1984.

Brennan, Charlie. "Walsh Family's Tragedy Brought to Life for Millions on Television." *Sun Sentinel,* Fla. October 11, 1983, p. 1,6A.

Bridge, Peter. "What Parents Should Do About Kiddie Porn." *Parents Magazine,* January 1978, p. 43.

Brisgone, Gina. "Slain Boy's Father Speaks Out Against Abuse." *The News Times,* Danbury, Conn. July 12, 1984, p. 1.

Bullough, Vern L. *The History of Prostitution.* New Hyde Park, New York: University Books, Inc., 1964.

Burgess, A. W., A. N. Groth, L. L. Holstrom and S. M. Sgroi. *Sexual Assault of Children and Adolescents.* Lexington Books, 1978.

Caldwell, Jean. "Protecting Your Children From Sexual Abuse." *American Baby Magazine,* March 1984, pp. 28, 30, 31, 36, 37, 62.

Capuzzo, Mike. "Kid-print Plans Proving Popular." The *Miami Herald,* Miami, Fla., March 25, 1983, p. 5BR.

Carroll, Susan. "Shoulder to Shoulder Pornography Fight Pledged." The *United Methodist Reporter,* September 21, 1984, p. 4.

Carter, Bill, interview. Spokesman for Bureau of Investigation, National Crime Information Center, Washington, D.C. NCIC computer entry information.

Child Guard. Parents Manual, American Federation of Police, Washington, D.C., 1983.

Clanton, Boots. "Father of Murdered Boy Seeks Rights for Missing Children." *North Myrtle Beach Times,* South Carolina. May 23, 1984, pp. 1–2.

Clinkscales, John and Louise. "Action Booklet." Seventh printing 1984. LaGrange, Georgia, pp. 30–42, 46–48.

———. LaGrange, Georgia. "The History of Find Me, Inc.," 1984.

———. "Family Reunion Month, Mother's Day Through Father's Day." 1983.

———. "Have You Forgotten Us? No, We Haven't Forgotten You!" 1983.

Clinkscales, John Dixon. "Kyle's Story, Friday Never Came. The Search for Missing People." *Vantage Press,* 1981.

Cohen, Michele. "Walsh Says Molesters Can Easily Find Teaching Jobs." Florida Report, *Sun Sentinel,* February 7, 1984, p. 8A.

Collins, Glen. "Study Finds Child Abduction by Parents Exceeds Estimates." The *New York Times,* October 23, 1983.

Congressional Record, proceedings and debates of the 98th Congress, First session. Senate Joint Resolution 94, Family Reunion Month. Vol. 129, No. 60, Washington, May 5, 1983.

Cummings, Priscilla. "Waiting for Jamie." *Woman's World, The Woman's Weekly,* August 14, 1984, p. 10.

Darrach, Brad and Dr. Joel Norris. "Serial Murderers, An American Tragedy." *Life* Magazine, August, 1984, pp. 58–74.

Dart, Bob. "A Grieving Family Lobbies for Missing Children." *San Francisco Chronicle,* April 24, 1984, p. 15.

Davidson, Howard A. "Sexual Exploitation of Children, an Overview of its Scope, Impact and Legal Ramifications." *FBI Law Enforcement Bulletin,* Office of Congressional and Public Affairs, Washington, D.C., February 1984, pp. 26–31.

Davis, Alexa, interview. Mother of children in attempted kidnapping. Midland, Texas, August 1984.

DiNova, Betty. "Absentee Reporting System," 1983.

———. "Block Parent Program," 1983.

———. "Educational Report No. 5, Federal Legislation," 1983.

———. "Educational Update Report No. 4."

———. "Kidnap Control Concept," 1984.

———. "Statistics Report No. 4," 1984.

———. "History of the Dee Scofield Awareness Program, Inc.," 1984.

———. "Vanished Child Agency List," 1984.

———. "What to Do if Your Child Disappears," 1983.

———. "Voluntary Fingerprint Sessions." All from Dee Scofield Awareness Program, Inc., Tampa, Florida.

———. "What Can an Officer Do in a Missing Child Case?" *Police Times,* Vol. 22, Number 6, September 1983.

Dinsdale, Katherine. "Somebody Stole My Baby." *Womans Day,* August 1, 1984, pp. 28–32.

Dodson, Dr. Fitzhugh with Paula Reuben. "How to Grandparent," *New American Library,* New York, 1981, pp. 151–2.

Dullea, Georgia. "Child Prostitution: Causes Are Sought." The *New York Times,* September 4, 1979, p. C11.

Elique, Lt. Jose A. "The Juvenile Runaway Phenomenon, a Law Enforcement Agencies Unique Approach." *FBI Law Enforcement Bulletin,* Office of Congressional and Public Affairs, Washington, D.C., February 1984, pp. 2–6.

Epstein, Sue. "Police Ordered to Move Fast on Reports of Missing Children." The *Star Ledger,* Newark, N.J., June 12, 1984, pp. 1, 12.

Escobar, Yolanda Rodriguez-, interview. Child protective services specialist. Texas Department of Human Resources, San Antonio, Texas, subject: Signs of Sexual Abuse.

FBI Law Enforcement Bulletin, The Missing Children's Act. Office of Congressional and Public Affairs. January 1984, pp. 17–21.

Gager, Nancy and Cathleen Schurr. *Sexual Assault: Confronting Rape in America.* New York, Grosset and Dunlap, 1976.

Gaysweek. "9 Men Indicted in Los Angeles for Running an International Child Prostitution Ring That Allegedly Used Children as Young as Four," August 21, 1978.

Gerber, Densen, Judianne and Stephen F. Hutchinson. "Child Prostitution and Child Pornography." International conference on legal aspects of health care for children. Toronto, Ontario, Canada, October 1979, p. 3.

Goldstein, Seth L. "Investigating Child Sexual Exploitation: Law Enforcement's Role." *FBI Law Enforcement Bulletin,* Washington, D.C., Office of Congressional and Public Affairs, pp. 22–30.

Groller, Ingrid. "Where Are They?", *Parents Magazine,* April 1981, p. 70.

Groth, Nicholas A. *Men Who Rape: The Psychology of the Offender.* Plenum Press, 1979.

Harmon, Rick. "Missing." The *Birmingham News,* Birmingham, Alabama, November 14, 1982.

Harvey, Lt. Jim, interview. Kerrville Police Department, Kerrville, Texas, 1984.

Haskell, Molly. *From Reverence to Rape.* New York: Holt, Rinehart & Winston, 1974.

Hawes, Bill, interview. Subject: Puppet Productions. "The McGruff Elementary School Puppet Program," San Diego, California, September 1984.

Hawkins, Paula. News from Paula Hawkins, United States Senator. "Hearing on Multiple Murders," opening statement of Senator Hawkins, July 12, 1983.

Henry, Waights G. "Has Anyone Seen Kyle Clinkscales Lately?", The *Sunday Ledger-Enquirer,* Columbus, GA, August 7, 1983, p. B-10.

Huebner, Carolyn, interview. President of Texas Child Search, San Antonio, Texas, August, 1984.

James, J. and J. Meyerding. "Early Sexual Experience and Prostitution." *American Journal of Psychiatry,* December, 1977.

Johnson, Randy and Tana Johnson. "Are You Raising a Victim?" *FBI Law Enforcement Bulletin,* Office of Congressional and Public Affairs, Washington, D.C., February 1984, pp. 10–14.

Karlin, Arno. *Sexuality and Homosexuality.* New York: W. W. Norton, 1971, p. 130.

LaGrange Daily News, LaGrange, GA. Staff: "John Clinkscales: A Man With a Mission." October 4, 1983, p. 7.

LaGrange Daily News, LaGrange, GA. Staff: "Kyle's Story to Be Told in New Book." October 23, 1980, p. 1.

LaGrange Daily News, LaGrange, GA. Staff: "Reagan Lauds Clinkscales in Oval Office." June 27, 1984, p. 1.

Lamb, Robert. "Whatever Happened to Kyle Clinkscales?" *Atlanta Constitution*, Atlanta, GA, May 9, 1981, pp. 1A, 4A.

Landers, Ann. "Treatment Center for Child Prostitutes." *New York Daily News*, February 26, 1979, p. 38.

Linebaugh, Patti. "How to Help Prevent a Child from Being Molested." The Children's Guardian. What To Do If Your Child Has Been Molested? SLAM (Societies League Against Molestation), Chino, CA, 1983.

Linedecker, Cliff. "Parents of Missing Son Push for National Family Reunion Month." *National Examiner*, July 10, 1984.

Margulies, Lee. " 'Adam' Points up TV's Power." *Calendar, Los Angeles Times*, March 15, 1984, pp. 1,12.

McCaslin, John. "Reagan Opens Missing Child Center." The *Washington Times*, Washington, D.C., June 14, 1984.

McPartlend, Kevin C. "Sexual Trauma Team, The Norfolk Experience." *FBI Law Enforcement Bulletin*, Office of Congressional and Public Affairs, Washington, D.C., February 1984, pp. 7–9.

Meddis, Sam. "Bill Forms Dragnet to Hunt Child Killers." *U.S.A. Today*, Thursday, October 27, 1983.

The *Miami Herald*, Miami, Fla. Staff: "President Signs Missing Kids Bill, Spurred by Adam Walsh Slaying." October 13, 1982.

Missing Children's Assistance Act (S. #2014), sponsored by Senator Paula Hawkins (R–Fla.) and Senator Arlen Specter (R–Pa.).

National Center for Missing and Exploited Children. Pamphlet on organization. 1835 K Street N.W., Suite 700, Washington, D.C. 20006.

National Crime Prevention Council and the Advertising Council, Inc. "McGruff's Take a Bite Out of Crime." Elementary School Puppet Program Booklet.

National Crime Prevention Council. "More Help: Films, Books, Child Assault Prevention." 805 15th Street, N.W., Room 718, Washington, D.C. 20005.

National Crime Prevention Council. "Resources Sheet, Physical and Sexual Child Abuse Centers." 805 15th Street, N.W., Room 718, Washington, D.C. 20005.

National Geographic World. "RRRR. . .RRRRR. . .Robots!" September, 1984, pp. 5–9.

National News of the American Legion Auxiliary. "Missing." March'April, 1984, pp. 10–12.

Parker, Jim. "Taped Testimony Approved in Molestation Trial." Regional, The *News and Courier*, Charleston, S.C., July 18, 1984, p. 10–B.

Peck, Jon. "House Passes Teacher Fingerprint Bill to Protect Children." The *Sun-Tattler*, Broward County, May 8, 1984, p. 4A.

Plotsker-Herman, Candace. "Raising Children in a Less-Than-Perfect World." *American Baby Magazine*, September 1984, pp. 61–73, 72, 80–81.

Press, Robert M. "Secrecy in Child Pornography Thwarts Law Enforcement." *Christian Science Monitor*, May 26, 1982, p. 9.

Raine, G. "End of a Terrible Ordeal." *Newsweek*, 102:48, November 21, 1983.

Readers Digest. Condensed from *Newsweek*, "Child Molesting: The Sad New Facts of Life." September 1984, pp. 148–152.

Rush, Florence. *The Best Kept Secret: Sexual Abuse of Children*. Englewood Cliffs, N.J., Prentice-Hall, Inc. 1980.

Russell, Diana E. H. *The Politics of Rape*. New York: Stein and Day. 1975.

Sanford, Linda Tschirhart. *The Silent Children: A Parents Guide to the Prevention of Child Sexual Abuse.* McGraw-Hill Book Company, Reprinted by arrangement with Anchor Press/Doubleday. 1980.

"Sexual Abuse of Children—Causes, Diagnoses and Management." *Pediatric Annual.* October 1984, Vol. 13, No. 10, pp. 753–58.

Sgroi, S. M. *A Handbook of Clinical Intervention in Child Sexual Abuse.* Lexington Books, 1981.

Skousen, W. Cleon. *So You Want to Raise a Boy.* Garden City, New York, 1962, pp. 152, 170, 171, 279–83.

Swift, C. "Sex Between Adults and Children." *The Journal of Psych-history,* Winter, 1977.

The Church of Jesus Christ of Latter-Day Saints. Family Home Evening Resource Book. Salt Lake City, Utah, 1983, pp. 272, 164, 243.

Time. "A Senator Recalls a Wrong (P. Hawkins Disclosure)." Vol. 123:27, May 7, 1984.

Tyler, R. P. "Toby." Child Pornography: The International Exploitation of Children. Fourth International Congress of Child Abuse and Neglect, Paris, France, September 9, 1982, p. 1.

United States Postal Services News, Washington, D.C. 20260–3100. "Crime Prevention Stamp to Be Issued September 26." August 5, 1984.

Walsh, Adam Child Resource Center. "Current Florida Statutes Suggested for Other States."

———. "Six Month Court Monitor Report, Wheels of Justice Turn Slowly for Child Molesters."

———. "Proposed Florida Legislation." All from Mercedes Executive Park, Ft. Lauderdale, Fla.

Weiss, Michael J. "Child Molesting—What Must Be Done to Protect Our Children." *Ladies Home Journal,* November 1984, pp. 114–202.

Woodhouse, Barbara. *No Bad Dogs.* The Woodhouse Ways, Summit Books, N.Y. Simon and Schuster, 1982, pp. 106–109.

Wissink, Stephen. "Missing Kids Get More Aid on Their Day." The *Sun-Tattler,* Broward County, Florida, May 25, 1984, pp. 1, 7A.

Index